A CALL TO ACTION

AN ANALYSIS AND OVERVIEW OF THE UNITED STATES CRIMINAL JUSTICE SYSTEM, WITH RECOMMENDATIONS

A CALL TO ACTION

AN ANALYSIS AND OVERVIEW OF THE UNITED STATES CRIMINAL JUSTICE SYSTEM, WITH RECOMMENDATIONS

The National Commission on Crime and Justice

Linda M. Thurston, Editor

Third World Press • Chicago

A CALL TO ACTION

Edited by Linda M. Thurston

First Edition
First Printing
1993

ISBN: 0-88378-067-4
Library of Congress #: 91-068516

Cover design by Craig A. Taylor

Manufactured in the United States of America

Third World Press
7822 South Dobson
Chicago, IL 60619

MEMBERS OF THE NATIONAL COMMISSION ON CRIME AND JUSTICE
1501 Cherry Street, Philadelphia, PA 19102
(215) 241-7130

Toney Anaya
Sante Fe, NM. Former Attorney General and Governor of New Mexico.

Clyde H. Bellcourt
Minneapolis, MN. Co-Founder, American Indian Movement.

Congressman John Conyers
Washington, DC. Chair, Criminal Justice Braintrust, Congressional Black Caucus.

Judge Nelson Diaz
Philadelphia, PA. Administrative Judge, Trial Division, Court of Common Pleas, Philadelphia.

Dr. L. C. Dorsey
Mound Bayou, MS. Public health administrator. Anti-death penalty and prisoner rights activist.

Carol Edmo
Portland, OR. Public Defenders Office. Advocate for alternatives to incarceration.

Isabel Garcia
Tuscon, AR. National Network for Immigration and Refugee Rights.

Prof. Alice P. Green
Albany, NY. Legislative Director, New York State Civil Liberties Union.

Richard Hatcher
Gary, IN. Former Mayor of Gary, Indiana. Chairman, African American Summit.

Jacquie Holmes
Portland, OR. Prisoner family advocate.

Rev. Bernice King
Atlanta, GA. Martin Luther King Center for Non-Violent Social Change.

Prof. Haki Madhubuti
Chicago, IL. Author and poet. Publisher of Third World Press. Director of the Gwendolyn Brooks Center, Chicago State University.

Benjamin Malcolm
New York, NY. Director, Parole Services of America. Former Commissioner of Corrections for New York City.
Esther Nieves
Chicago, IL. Former Executive Director, Chicago Mayor's Advisory Committee on Latino Affairs.
Walter Ridley
Washington, DC. Director, District of Columbia Department of Corrections.
Dr. Rick St. Germaine
Eau Claire, WI. Professor of Education, University of Wisconsin.
Bill Tamayo
San Francisco, CA. Managing Attorney, Asian Law Caucus.
Dr. James Turner
Ithaca, NY. Chairman Emeritus, Africana Studies and Research Center, Cornell University.
Carl Upchurch
Newark, OH. President, Progressive Prisoners Movement.
Rev. S. Mike Yasutake
Evanston, IL. Director, Interfaith Prisoners of Conscience Project, National Council of Churches, USA.

STAFF FOR THE COMMISSION
Linda M. Thurston, Coordinator
Ron Daniels, Consultant
Charyn Sutton, Consultant

CONTENTS

FOREWORD

The 1971 uprising at Attica Correctional Facility placed
the prison movement for reform and prisoners' rights on the
front pages of newspapers across the nation. Attica, after
twenty years, is still being argued in the courts. Few who
followed the Black-led rebellion can forget the hurricane of
state troopers and guards on September 13, rushing like dogs in
heat to retake the prison under the muted shouts of "save me a
nigger." Malcolm Bell's *The Turkey Shoot* documents that
horrible episode and its attempted cover-up.[1] Attica is the
perfect metaphor for 200 years of prison misdevelopment in the
United States: prisons don't work.

According to Lee H. Bowker's *Prison Victimization*, the
prison system in the United States is modern slavery, and those
who suffer the greatest are African Americans and other people
of color.[2] It is now common knowledge that in the American
criminal justice system, money talks and everybody else does
time. The major people involved in criminal activity in

America are not people of color but white men. Yet a survey of prison and jail inhabitants will reveal that these institutions have become the final answer for the victims of poverty, mentally and culturally different, inadequately educated, un-employed and non-white.

According to the National Institute of Justice, in states with large inner city populations, the percentage of incarcerated persons who are African American is 83 percent. The one-in-four figure of Black males involved in the criminal justice system, documented by the Sentencing Project of Washington, DC will surely double for the age group 18 to 29 if current trends continue.[3] This does not even include the 66 percent of women behind bars who are African American.

That over 60 percent of the prison population is poor and of color only confirms for the thinking person that if one wishes to indulge in serious crime in America, it is best to earn an MBA or law degree. The Savings and Loans bandits and their kind do not go to Attica-like facilities but to "country clubs with fences and tennis courts"—if they are incarcerated at all. It is common political wisdom that anything goes in America as long as one does not get caught. From Panama to Iraq to the cities of the heartland, America's capacity to destroy lives has been documented. Yet, the call from overzealous politicians is to build bigger prisons, more prisons and harsher prisons, not for the multi-million dollar criminals of America, but for the dispossessed.

The call for increased imprisonment is in keeping with the short-sighted economic development for states from Michigan to California, where prison building and staffing is big busi-ness. In the federal anti-crime package of 1989, President Bush proposed spending $1.2 billion—with $1 billion for the construction of new federal prisons to house 24,000 additional prisoners. Private enterprise also has gotten into the act. The WRI Group of Shreveport, Louisiana, has proposed to build prisons in East Texas for the sole purpose of importing prisoners from over-crowded areas like the District of Columbia, California and New York State.[4]

Currently, the criminal justice system is a $35 billion industry. Future profits from privatization of prisons could be enormous. Projections are that with states paying anywhere from $28 to $65 per day per prisoner, investors could recoup their money in less than ten years and turn the prisons over to the states after 20 years with ten years of clear profits. This type of arrangement will allow investors to earn substantial returns on their investment, profits that will likely go untaxed because of special arrangements with local municipalities.

Local politicians are listening to these ideas as an alternative to passing bond proposals and building prisons with tax dollars. The projects are especially popular in states with large urban populations where existing prisons are already over-crowded and arrests and convictions of persons of color are continuing at a break-neck pace. For example, in Louisiana there are 15,000 outstanding warrants; in California, over 30,000 outstanding warrants; and in the city of Chicago, approximately 25,000.[5]

To understand prisons in American society, it is not only necessary to make distinctions between right and wrong, good and evil, lawful and unlawful. We must also look at poverty and fear, politics and economy, race and racism. It is clear that the roots of crime lie deep in the social structure and culture of this country. The current attitude toward incarceration is a "lock them up, bury the key" mentality. This attitude is a cancer in the blood and, like polluted water, is deadly to us all. We recognize that for many of those in prisons, a connection to family and community is missing in their lives, while an allegiance to America's negative values is present. For African Americans, Latinos, Asian Americans, Native Americans and others, life in the United States is like walking barefoot on razor sharp rolled wire. Prisons cannot heal those wounds. In fact, the mistreatment of prisoners while incarcerated does not lead to rehabilitation, but, rather to a greater propensity for criminal activity for many.

Certainly the cost of ignorance is high, and as a nation we will continue to get into debt as long as all we do is talk about the problems and lock people up.

That is why this *Call to Action* must be more than just talk. It must serve as a document for mobilization and change. Certainly it will have failed in its mission if it serves only to soothe the conscience of a few as the others self-righteously file it away with the hundreds of other studies that dare to indict the inhumane treatment of men, women and children by America's legal-economic-racist system. Until and unless we address the social problems of America, crime will rage unabated in our streets. A dysfunctional culture produces dysfunctional people. The solutions to our problems of crime lie not in prisons but in providing for all people a way to productively live their lives. *A Call to Action* speaks to solutions.

Haki R. Madhubuti
Commission Member
The National Commission on Crime and Justice

INTRODUCTION

In January 1990, the National Commission on Crime and Justice was convened by the 200 Years of the Penitentiary Project of the American Friends Service Committee. This independent commission was unique in that its membership was drawn entirely from communities of color in the United States—African American, Latino, Asian/Pacific and Native American. As co-chairs of this commission, we faced the challenging task of hearing testimony, reading letters and articles and deliberating on major issues facing the criminal justice system in this time of crisis.

The disproportionate rate of imprisonment and its devastating affects on communities of color has been widely discussed. Yet the voices of the people in these communities are seldom heard in the debate on issues concerning crime and justice. Included among the Commission's membership are community leaders, criminal justice administrators (including current and former corrections department directors), activists working for the rights of political prisoners, immigrants and refugees, youth activists, members of the clergy, victims of crime, persons who have served time in prison, family members of those currently in prison, scholars, attorneys, current and former elected officials, writers and health professionals. These women and men bring a wealth of experience and insight to our analysis of the extent the justice system impacts their respective communities as well as the country.

Over a one and a half year period the Commission toured the prison in Lorton, Virginia, held public hearings in Atlanta and Philadelphia and held a third hearing inside the prison at Greenhaven, New York. (Additional hearings were planned in Chicago and Los Angeles, but were cancelled for lack of funding.) Commission members have reviewed research materials on a wide range of topics, including sentencing, drug and alcohol treatment, employment in prisons, prisons as industry, women in prison, families of prisoners, AIDS and other prison health care issues, reconciliation and mediation programs, community-based corrections, and the particular challenges faced by African Americans, Latinos, Asian/Pacific Americans and Native Americans in their interactions with the justice system. Meetings were convened to review these materials and to discuss concrete strategies for change in the justice system.

With a clear recognition of recent news reports on violent crime and increasing prison populations as well as this country's long history of repressive prisons, courts, and police departments, the Commission worked to develop a clear analysis of the country's responses to crime and the impact of those responses on the poor and people of color.

This report reflects a wide range of experience and opinion, drawing upon both the information gathered from these outside sources and from the diversity of the Commission itself. The report is entitled *A Call to Action* because it is intended as a challenge to the criminal justice system, the general public and communities of color to make fundamental changes in this nation's responses to crime. The findings and recommendations address the need to focus on the root causes of crime as well as the workings of the criminal justice system itself—police, courts, prisons and post-release services. However, the major focus of the Commission's report is on the need for change in the prison system and in the way in which criminal justice system facilities are used.

The Commission, in its research, deliberations, findings and recommendations, offers a vision of a criminal justice system that does not rely first and foremost upon imprisonment, but utilizes a range of means to insure both public safety and individual and community responsibility for crime prevention and response. With these findings and recommendations, the Commission challenges groups and individuals, particularly policy makers and elected officials, to begin to really "fight crime" by creating a justice system that is truly just making our communities safer and more whole. Certainly the perspectives incorporated in this document are in some ways "colored" by the insight and experiences of the racial and ethnic groups represented on the Commision: African American, Asian/Pacific American, Latino and Native American.

Isabel Garcia, J.D., Co-chair
L.C. Dorsey, D.S.W., Co-chair
The National Commission on Crime and Justice

I

BACKGROUND OF THE CRISIS

In 1990, as the National Commission on Crime and Justice began its work, news reports were full of accounts of increasing violent crime, national prison populations, and disproportionate imprisonment of the poor and people of color.

The escalation of crime did not occur in a vacuum. Reaganomics caused dramatic cuts in federal budgets for social programs. At the state and local levels, fewer resources were available for education, housing, jobs and health care (including drug abuse treatment). This, combined with an influx of crack-cocaine, contributed to the increase in crime. A hopelessness began to permeate poor neighborhoods and communities of color throughout the United States that was reflected in a drug-induced escapism of anger through violence. As the death toll began to rise in many communities and people became increasingly victimized by and aware of violent crime, calls for vengeance and punishment increased. In hopes of gaining empowerment and affecting change, community residents became advocates for "Law and Order."

The concept of "Law and Order" has been a common refrain throughout much of American history. It helped create former President Richard M. Nixon's landslide victory in 1968 and returned again 20 years later in the form of Willie Horton political commercials that ushered President George Bush into the White House. Woven into the fabric of this slogan is a clear identification of race as a facet of criminal behavior. Just as there was no doubt in the public mind that the "Law and Order" approach of Nixon would keep people of color in line, so too the Willie Horton television advertisements played strongly on the supposed color of crime in America.

The War on Drugs also has been waged along the color line. This "war" continues to be directed disproportionately against persons of color even though the majority of drug users and the major kingpins of the international drug trade are white. Police have instituted humiliating public search-and-seizure procedures in communities of color, forcibly evicted the families of persons suspected of using drugs and coordinated neighborhood campaigns which merely shifted illegal drug selling from one corner to the next. No real attention has been given to attacking high level supply or community level demand. Despite the clear relationship between drug abuse and crime, there has been relatively little funding for drug abuse prevention and treatment programs and services. Instead, 70 percent of the new federal anti-drug funds were allocated to pay for more police, more prison cells and more courts.

Unfortunately, this nation's response to crime in the 1990s is not appreciably different from its responses 200 years ago when the penitentiary system was initiated. Even though the evidence is clear that imprisonment does not end crime or rehabilitate criminals, the United States remains committed to incarceration as its first line of defense against crime and violence.

It is now widely believed that responding to crime by locking up persons convicted or accused of crimes is essentially flawed because it relies primarily upon punishment and restriction. Those who oppose widespread use of incarceration, including most members of the Commission, feel that it is fairer and more effective to ensure restitution to the victim and to provide "corrective" education, treatment and training to convicted persons. Long-term incarceration should be used for the very few convicted persons who actually pose a constant threat to the safety of the community.

The Commission believes that the emphasis on incarceration is counter-productive and cannot be allowed to continue. Communities of color are losing too much talent to the round-robin of jails and prisons. Without concentrating on the root causes of crime—which include joblessness, alcoholism and drug abuse, illiteracy and homelessness—there is little chance that the cycle of mass imprisonment will end. Furthermore, the drain on public resources that has occurred with the expansion of criminal sanctions threatens the funding for schools, health centers, job training, higher education and other beneficial programs.

Clearly, the criminal justice establishment must make substantive changes. However, the Commission believes that the primary impetus for those changes must come from those who suffer most from its present pratices — communities of color. The United States must find ways to work toward a criminal justice system that will rely less on incarceration, especially maximum-security incarceration, and more on addressing the true needs of victims of crime and persons convicted of crime. There must be a recognition that if funds are expended on correcting the inequities in American society, crime rates will decrease. Conversely, as long as society continues to relegate individuals to lives of poverty, illiteracy and racial/ethnic discrimination, crime levels will be unacceptably high in this nation.

Providing a person in prison with an education and job training will not keep him or her from committing crimes against property if there is no job available following release. Teaching prison guards about the importance of cultural diversity and the positive contributions of all races and ethnic groups will not be effective if the overwhelming majority of persons in the upper-level management of prison systems is white and the prisoners are primarily persons of color.

The Commission feels strongly that the crisis of this nation's criminal justice system must be addressed in a three-pronged attack:

1.   Major changes must be made in the current delivery systems for policing, sentencing, prison, probation and parole to assure that the criminal justice system does more than simply punish persons convicted of crimes. Rather, these systems must help convicted persons to become reestablished as productive members of their communities, through the development of effective alternatives to incarceration.

2.   Significant attention must be given to the root causes of crime—including joblessness, racial and ethnic discrimination, illiteracy—with a substantial commitment of financial and human resources from the public and

private sectors.

3.   Communities of color must recognize the need to establish community-based mechanisms which provide programs for youth, assist victims of crimes and facilitate the reintegration of reformed and rehabilitated ex-prisoners as positive, contributing members of the community.

This call to action of the National Commission on Crime and Justice provides a perspective on each of these three components and makes thirty-nine recommendations for change. The Commission believes that these recommendations can help to create a criminal justice system that can truly justify the use of the word "justice" in its title and, more importantly, can ensure local communities throughout the United States much less threatening rates of crime and violence.

II
ANALYSIS OF CRIME AND
JUSTICE IN AMERICA

═══════════

The diversity of this nation, in terms of its racial and ethnic mix and the varying levels of income and social status, requires a criminal justice system that has more complexity than "lock 'em up and throw away the key." Yet, far too often, that is the approach taken. Politicians win elections with pledges to take tax money from schools and use those funds to build jails. Ex-prisoners are branded with "scarlet letters" and isolated from the mainstream community as unsociable, unemployable and untrustworthy.

The Commission identified as a fundamental failing of the criminal justice system its commitment to the concept of "exile" as punishment for wrongdoing. This translates into an overall inability of the system to reintegrate persons convicted of crimes back into society. Certainly there are some individuals who have been "rehabilitated,"* but this has tended to occur in spite of the criminal justice system rather than because of it. The belief in exile is a central tenet of the American criminal justice system. The concept is rooted in the recognition that separation from family, friends and community is a severe form of punishment. Furthermore, by exiling wrongdoers, the community would be protected from "different" or "threatening" individuals. Because these concepts undergird the entire criminal justice system, attempts at reintegration of convicted persons meet strong resistance. Indeed, the commitment to exile is so ingrained that it continues long after the formal sentence has been served.

Another major failing of the criminal justice system that the Commission identified is the rigidity and slowness of the system in responding to new and different situations. In the 200 years since the founding of the penitentiary system, little has really changed. Prison systems that were created to incarcerate adult men now have increasing numbers of women and juveniles, yet have not made adjustments to better address the needs of those distinct populations. Prison systems that once had heroin addicts now have crack addicts, but few modifications have been made in recognition of the major differences in these

---

* The term "rehabilitation" will be used in this document to describe the process of returning a prisoner back to his or her community as a whole person. Use of this term is tempered by the recognition that some within the criminal justice system prefer the term "habilitated" because they believe the use of the prefix "re" implies a return to a positive home and community life-style that for most incarcerated persons never existed. It also recognizes that some individuals also reject the term for its implications that being rehabilitated means turning away from personal beliefs and accepting without debate the essential tenets of Americanism.

addictive substances. Prison systems that had virtually all English-speaking populations now have persons with many native languages and distinctive cultures, yet the guards have little or no training in handling such diversity.

In the face of such a rapidly changing environment, most prison systems have retrenched and gone "back to basics." Rather than being more open to innovation and modification, prison systems have become more closed and resistant to major, systemic changes. Those modifications that are made tend to be piecemeal, limited in scope and designed to reinforce the core design of incarceration, punishment and retribution.

RACE AND RACISM

The United States has the highest rates of incarceration in the world.[6] Yet even within this country, the rates vary widely from jurisdiction to jurisdiction and by race and ethnicity. For example, incarceration rates for American whites are similar to the relatively low rates in European nations. However, for African Americans, incarceration rates parallel those of South Africa, a white-controlled African nation that has become a pariah throughout the world for its racism and reliance on prisons and jails and public policy.[7]

Persons of color throughout America continue to be singled out unfairly in this nation's criminal justice system. Prisons in the Midwest have a highly disproportionate number of Native Americans. In the West, there is a growing fear of Asian street gangs. In the Southeast and along the Mexico-United States border, Latinos are blamed for the influx of drugs. There is a commonality in each of these instances. The color of the alleged criminal becomes more important than the crime. Indeed, the race and ethnicity of the criminal often "colors" the crime such that the crimes committed by African Americans, Asian Americans*, Latinos and Native Americans of lower socioeconomic status are treated more harshly than crimes committed by middle and upper-class European Americans.

Recently, most of the attention has been focused on the numbers of Black males in prison—particularly in the wake of the 1990 Sentencing Project Report, which documented that nearly one out of every four Black men ages 20 to 29 were in prison or on probation or parole. Yet, the polarization around the issue is such that opposing sides pointed to the statistic as "proof" of their position. Advocates for criminal justice system reform saw in those statistics validation for their position that the criminal justice system is racist at its core. Others felt, incorrectly, that the numbers actually demonstrated some innate violence and criminality on the part of African Americans, particularly African American men. While the Willie Horton commercials and the Sentencing Project Report have focused attention on African American men and the criminal justice system, the actual crisis is much broader—involving the spectrum of persons of color in this country, including women and juveniles.

The primacy of race in any discussion of this country's criminal justice system is, or should be, immediately recognized. Even though many of the early White settlers were

---

* Except in Hawaii, Asian Americans represent the exception to this statement. Statistics from state and local jurisdictions indicate that Japanese, Chinese and Filipinos tend to be underrepresented at all levels of the criminal justice system—prison, probation and parole. However, with a poverty rate of 14 percent—twice that of Whites— it is expected that more Asians, especially those from Vietnam and other parts of Southeast Asia, will be involved in the criminal justice system.

fleeing from certain or possible imprisonment in Europe, the complexion of imprisonment in the United States has always been disproportionately non-white.

Africans were brought to America as property and, as such, had no real standing before courts. Free Blacks were covered by "Black Codes" which stipulated a different and restricted form of "justice." While the laws varied from jurisdiction to jurisdiction, there were few places where an African could go to have a fair hearing. This was demonstrated most dramatically in the Dred Scott decision, where the United States Supreme Court concluded that Americans of African descent were not citizens and had no true legal rights which government or individuals were bound to respect.

The racism that was part of this nation's criminal justice system at its inception has continued. Even when slavery was abolished, the concept of forced, unpaid labor was permitted in America's prisons and jails. The predominantly Black Southern "chain gangs" became slavery's logical extension. Even today, African Americans are far more likely than any other group to be placed in jail or prison. In the 1970s, William Nagel found that states with large non-white populations (even those with low crime rates) have large prison populations. "There is no significant correlation between a state's racial composition and its crime rate," he wrote, "but there is a very great positive relationship between its racial composition and its incarceration rate."[8]

Blacks are not the only ones who have suffered race-based justice in this nation. Asians have faced racial discrimination in the United States since Chinese men were first brought to this country in the 1850s to provide cheap labor for the building of the railroads. In 1882, the immigration of Chinese laborers was suspended. Japanese immigration was terminated by Congress in 1924. Other Asians also faced discrimination, even those who came from the Phillippines, a United States colony. For many years, Asians were prevented from becoming naturalized citizens; only their children born in the United States could qualify for citizenship.[9]

During World War II, anti-Asian hostility reached its peak with the incarceration, without hearings or trials, of more than 120,000 persons of Japanese ancestry in concentration camps. Two-thirds of those incarcerated were United States citizens. Many of the others had lived in the United States since the early 1900s. Although the United States was also at war with Germany and Italy, persons of German and Italian ancestry were not similarly incarcerated.

The criminal justice system's treatment of Native Americans has also been abysmal. The first prisons in many of the Western territories that comprised the American "frontier" were stockades built to imprison Native Americans who fought against the capture of their lands and displacement of their people. As with the African Americans and Asians, the concept of allowing Native Americans to have "citizenship" in what has become the United States was a difficult concept for the white settlers to accept.

These early prisons were brutal places which held individuals who were not seen as prisoners of war but rather as savages who were less than human. These "Indian" stockades metamorphosed into the prison systems of these territories, bringing along not only the physical structures but the philosophy of white racial superiority. Native Americans are vastly overrepresented in prison populations. In Minnesota, for example, Native American people make up less than one half of one percent of the total state population, but 15 percent of the adult prison population and as much as 35 percent of the juvenile population.[10]

While the United States has technically recognized some level of sovereignty or independence for Native American nations, virtually all legal treaties established with those nations have been ignored or broken over the years. As a result, individual Native Americans have been placed in a complex quandary regarding legal rights. Depending on the jurisdiction in which a crime was committed, on the nature of the crime itself and the affiliation of the person suspected of committing the crime, Native American criminal suspects can find their cases adjudicated by tribal, federal, state or county authorities. Because reservations are under the jurisdiction of the Federal Bureau of Indian Affairs, many crimes committed on Native American land are classified as federal crimes, and Native Americans are often, after conviction, sent to federal prisons for crimes that, if committed by anyone else, would result in a sentence at a state prison.

Latinos have also suffered under an Anglo criminal justice system. Mexicans and Puerto Ricans, who have battled for self-determination of their lands taken during wars of expansion and colonization, have been treated extremely harsh in United States courts and prisons. Self-determination claims are addressed by United States courts with little or no adherence to the sanctions of international law.

More recently, the focus on drug trafficking has given Latinos a new stereotype to fight against as the erroneous public perception grows that all or most Latinos, especially those who are poor, are somehow involved in drugs. The "war on drugs" has been used as a pretext to curb the due process of non-

European immigrants. Central American and Haitian refugees seeking asylum have been disproportionately incarcerated, in contrast to the treatment by immigration authorities of Eastern Europeans seeking asylum. Many Latinos are assumed to be undocumented and are insulted and humiliated at all levels of the criminal justice process. Police, prosecutors, guards and others are rarely fluent in Spanish, placing Latinos who do not speak English at an extreme disadvantage in negotiating a complex legal system that differs in many ways from the criminal justice systems in Mexico, Panama, Cuba and other Latin American countries.

The Commission's assessment of the criminal justice system draws heavily on the nature of race relations and discrimination in the United States as a way to define the issues and identify possible solutions. While recent articles have focused on the number of African American males in prison or on probation and parole, Latinos, Native Americans and some Asian groups also are found in prisons and jails in numbers far exceeding their representation in the population. The Commission believes strongly that there must be recognition of the racism that currently exists in the criminal justice system, followed by strong steps to bring about equality and fairness.

ECONOMICS AND EDUCATION
The racism within the criminal justice system is further complicated by economic and educational factors. Across all racial groups, prisoners are drawn from the poorest sectors of society. A large percentage are unemployed at the time of their arrest or have only sporadic employment. Of those with jobs, many have incomes near or below the poverty level. Most prisoners have not completed high school; many are function-

ally illiterate. In 1983, the average annual income of a person before incarceration was less than $6,000.[11]

Unfortunately, these problems are getting worse. The social and economic policies of the last decade caused an unprecedented increase in the numbers of people living in poverty in the United States, as well as a widening gap between the incomes and living standards of the rich and poor. Throughout this entire period, prison populations grew rapidly. With budgets slashed for every type of social service, prisons now stand out as the country's principle government program for the poor.

Most of the persons in the criminal justice system are there for economic crimes. Of those arrested in 1988, nearly 75 percent were accused of property offenses like burglary, larceny or automobile theft.[12] Poverty is the cause of crimes that would probably not be committed if those who are impoverished had the financial means necessary to provide their basic needs: food, clothing, shelter, education and healthcare. Women, in particular, are generally in jail for property crimes.[13] Poverty also diminishes one's access to fair treatment within the criminal justice system; in many instances poor people are punished disproportionately to the crimes that they commit.

This is not to say that all crimes are caused by poverty. Much of the white collar crime in this nation results from materialism, greed and corruption. Despite the loss of economic and material resources and the injury (and sometimes death) caused by white collar crime, these crimes are not punished as severely as crimes rooted in poverty. This nation's fascination with guns and other instruments of destruction means that arguments too frequently end in violence and bloodshed. Sexual abuse, child abuse and rape often have no direct economic motivations. Nonetheless, in looking at the crimes that lead to the majority of incarcerations, there is a clear correlation with socioeconomic status.

The United States already has more people in prison than any other country in the world.[14] Yet, this nation seeks to deal with overcrowded prisons by building new prisons and escalating crime rates by increasing mandatory sentences for crimes. The public continues to demand that criminals be jailed, whatever the nature of the crime, and continues to oppose the release of imprisoned persons—even those who are in jail awaiting trial because they are too poor to pay bail fees. There is widespread resistance to locating halfway houses, pre-release facilities, community correctional centers as well as drug and alcohol abuse treatment programs in local communities. This opposition does not only come from white, middle- and upper-class communities, some of the most heated opposition to "softening" punishment comes from communities of color which have, within their boundaries, the majority of victims of violent crimes.

The expectation seems to be that society will forever need prisons as a way of dealing with crime. Prisons have become a major industry in many parts of the country, particularly rural areas that have seen the departure of industry and the end of small family farms. This country now spends $35 billion each year on its criminal justice system and that amount continues to grow.[15] The number of prisoners seems to expand to meet the number of new prison cells available. Long periods of incarceration and capital punishment are seen as the most popular ways to reassure Americans that the crime issue is being addressed.

This emphasis on incarceration is not having its desired

effect, however. People do not feel safe, and crime continues to plague communities. That is why this nation must find ways to create a criminal justice system that will rely less on incarceration, especially maximum security incarceration, and more on addressing the true needs of victims of crime and persons convicted of crime.

It is clear that the criminal justice system is in need of major renovations. As long as society continues to relegate individuals to lives of poverty, illiteracy and racial/ethnic discrimination, crime levels will be unacceptably high in this nation. The Commission believes that if funds are expended on correcting the inequities in American society, crime rates will decrease.

III

STRUCTURE OF THE CRIMINAL JUSTICE SYSTEM

Persons of color and the poor are subject to disadvantages at every stage of the criminal justice process—arrest, pretrial release, prosecution, conviction, sentencing and parole release. The accumulation of disparate decisions made in the context of institutionalized racism results, ultimately, in more harsh sanctions for persons of color and the poor than for others who commit similar crimes. For instance, Black and Latino suspects are more likely to be arrested than white suspects, either because they are perceived to be more threatening or because their alleged crime is more visible. Also, the poor and persons of color are more likely than middle and upperclass white defendants to be detained pretrial. This is an important point because it has been shown that detention negatively affects trial outcome.

POLICING

The first encounter that most individuals have with the

criminal justice system is with the police. Within many
communities of color, there is considerable wariness regarding
the role of police and the perception that the role of the police
is to protect the property rights of whites rather than the
physical safety of community residents. As a result, residents
often hesitate to call police except in serious situations and then
complain that response time of police to these calls is seriously
delayed.

Often, police officers do not seem able to distinguish
between the victims of crimes and the perpetrators of crimes
within communities of color. This is particularly true for police
officers who are not knowledgeable about the cultural norms of
the communities to which they are assigned. Often individuals
are stopped, searched and even arrested because they "fit the
profile" of a drug dealer. African American and Latino
ministers, teachers, actors and athletes in expensive cars have
been stopped and harassed by police as part of drug dragnets
while similarly attired whites driving similar cars have not been
questioned.

Violence by police officers against individuals suspected
of crimes is another major issue of concern in communities of
color. The videotaped beating of traffic violation suspect
Rodney King by Los Angeles police in March 1991 drew
widespread national attention to the problem of police violence. Physical abuse of suspects by police, including some
documented cases of actual torture, is far more prevalent than
is generally recognized by the public. Police departments that
have as their basic credo "getting the bad guys" or "ridding the
streets of scum" are more likely to descend into police violence
than those that emphasize public and community service. On
the Mexico-United States border, the violence inflicted on the

border communities by the myriad of law enforcement agencies, including local police and Immigration and Naturalization Service (INS) officers, is so prevalent that the American Friends Service Committee has established a program, the Immigration Law Enforcement Monitoring Project, to document some of the abuses.

The Commission is aware that some police departments have attempted to reduce race and ethnic-based abusive actions by hiring more ethnic and racial minorities. This is a positive step. However, if hired into situations that reward institutional and individual racism, persons of color can find themselves either becoming part of long-standing racist and violent policing practices or leaving. Where there has been support for diversity from the highest levels of police management and/or support from rank and file organizations such as the National Black Police Association (NBPA) and the National Organization of Blacks in Law Enforcement (NOBLE), individual police have been able to confront racism more directly within the policing system.

Community Policing

The Commission feels that one of the ways that the policing function can be improved within communities of color is through community policing. The essence of this model is that police are seen as part of the day-to-day life of the neighborhood and not as an outside force that simply reacts to crimes and crises. A fundamental component of any community policing effort is the willingness of police departments to take seriously the community's definition of its crime problems and to involve community residents in solutions to those problems. In many neighborhoods, community policing ef-

forts include expansion of foot patrols, implementation of Two
Watch programs and establishment of police mini-stations in
high-crime areas. This model also requires that police develop
strong linkages with indigenous community leaders and local
service providers.[16] Studies have shown that community
policing "helps to provide citizens with a sense of control over
their police services and often fosters positive police-commu-
nity contact. The concept of police becomes associated with
community helpers rather than agents of social control."[17]

Community policing can serve to hold policing agencies
accountable in neighborhoods where community residents
perceive the police as a violent, occupying force, but one that
is needed to curb other kinds of criminal violence. In these
neighborhoods, people often feel torn between needing police
protection and recognizing the degree to which police seem to
view the entire community as criminal. Building respect,
accountability and trust between the community and police
through community policing can help reduce the tension.

Independent Monitoring and Community Review

While police departments can and should monitor the
actions of their staffs, external community-based oversight is
also important. Police work can be extremely stressful and
dangerous. The organizational culture of police departments
often encourages a "them" (criminals) against "us" (police)
mentality, increasing the tendency of individual officers to
respond inappropriately, with disrespect, lack of sensitivity
and even violence. Furthermore, police officers are often
exposed to opportunities for corruption. It is essential that
systems of accountability to the community be established
which allow for independent reviews of police conduct. Citi-

zens' review boards can perform this important monitoring task.

Development of additional training curricula that address cultural diversity and non-violent conflict resolution is essential to equip police officers to operate in the current environment. For example, behaviors that may seem anti-social to an individual of European background may be well within cultural norms for persons of African, Asian or Latin heritage. Police use of racial or ethnic slurs may add to the tension surrounding an arrest by causing increased resistance from a suspect and community residents. Racial and cultural sensitivity training and knowledge of cultural awareness can minimize these difficulties.

PROSECUTION AND SENTENCING

Like the police, the court system is an integral part of the criminal justice system. Despite the stated commitment of the government of the United States to due process, poor people and persons of color face major difficulties in obtaining justice through the courts. Persons who do not have sufficient financial resources have to depend on public defenders who are often overworked. Attorneys who represent indigent defendants brought to the attention of the commission the impossibility of providing adequate defense to clients without needed resources.[18] Public defenders offices invariably have too few attorneys, too few investigators, and too little funding. Parallel complaints come from defendants and their families, some of whom reported speaking to their attorneys for the first time only minutes before entering the court room.[19]

Court systems also must cope with the increasing ethnic and racial diversity of this nation. Individuals who are not literate in English or who come from nations with different legal traditions often do not understand the intricacies of the prosecution and sentencing processes. As a result, these individuals often agree to give up certain rights without fully understanding the implications. Juries are chosen from registered voters who are not reflective of the racial, ethnic and socioeconomic status of many defendants and, therefore, are not necessarily the peers of those on trial.

The severe overcrowding of many jails and prisons and the increased number of drug-related cases have added further stresses to court systems around the nation. In some instances, special drug courts have been established to deal with the backlog of drug-related cases and to address community complaints about drug dealers going free following arrests. Plea bargaining has increased, with more defendants being given the opportunity to plead guilty to a lesser charge in return for a reduced sentence. The Commission believes, however, that all individuals must be fully informed of their rights and not be pressured to waive those rights to increase conviction rates or lessen the backlog of cases. This is particularly important in the case of non-citizen defendants, for whom a plea bargain or conviction can have immigration consequences.

Court staff persons face serious difficulties in performing their duties in this current environment. Judges throughout the country told the Commission that they wanted more freedom to sentence offenders to non-incarcerative or less-incarcerative programs, but that such programs either did not exist in their jurisdictions or were not sufficiently publicized.[20]

Harsher Sentences
In response to public outcry about violent crime and

backlash against some plea bargaining arrangements, legislatures throughout the country have enacted new sentencing laws. In many instances, these laws call for longer, mandatory sentences that are not keyed to the circumstances of the crime or the conditions of the offender but to increasingly narrow definitions of particular offenses. Judges and district attorneys are often afraid to risk their elected seats on the bench by suggesting anything other than the harshest sentences. Harsher sentences are seen as a panacea, a guarantee that dangerous and violent people will be taken away from embattled communities and that violence in those communities will cease. These sentences present no "miracle cure" for crime because they do not have the deterrent effect claimed for them. Furthermore these harsher sentences fail to address the root causes of crime, and are often applied with more regard to race and economic status than to the delivery of justice.

There is some built-in level of conflict between justice systems which establish set terms for specific crimes and more flexible systems which, on the surface, allow more attention to extenuating circumstances. In theory, mandatory sentencing should eliminate differences based on ethnicity and socioeconomic status. Yet, distinctions are often built into the legislation — such as stiffer sentences for drugs which are used more often by Blacks than for drugs used more often by Whites. On the other hand, without set standards, the outcome of the criminal justice process can deviate widely for similar crimes committed by people of color and Whites. This is particularly true if the "justice" is administered within a racist context that favors Whites, persons with education and those with considerable financial resources.

The restriction of judicial discretion does not always

serve justice. Supporters of mandatory sentencing laws claim that these laws are designed to avoid the unfair bias of some judges. However mandatory sentencing also ties the hands of those judges committed to taking into account the life circumstances and experience of convicted persons brought before them for sentencing. Judges committed to finding alternatives to incarceration, for the benefit of the offender as well as to alleviate prison overcrowding, are far less able to construct sentences which do not rely upon imprisonment in jurisdictions that have mandatory sentencing laws.

Sentencing Considerations

The ability of a judge to determine an appropriate sentence is dependent on a series of factors. Unfortunately, many judges are given little information other than the nature of the crime on which to base a decision. There are efforts in some jurisdictions to include information about the impact of the crime on the victim as part of the sentencing process. This can be quite valuable in crafting restitution as part of the sentence if the defendant is found guilty.

The Commission feels, however, that it is also important for the judge to consider the impact of a potential sentence on another set of victims—the family of the convicted person. Often the incarceration of a convicted person has a major and long-standing negative impact on the spouse and dependent children, particularly if the convicted person has been providing the family with financial and emotional support. The inclusion of a family impact study as part of the pre-sentence investigation report can assist the judge in the sentencing decision. Also, judges should be provided with detailed information about the training, educational, health, treatment and counseling needs of convicted persons and the availability of programs to meet these needs within various criminal justice facilities and in the community.

The Commission heard repeated calls for better training of court staff, including judges. Because racist attitudes — a major factor in the disproportionately high sentences and high incarceration rates of people of color — thrive in an atmosphere of ignorance, there is a particular need for education on the culture, language and history of the populations in the system. There is also a need for education on the issues facing non-citizens, for whom the immigration consequences of a conviction can be more severe than the criminal punishment. Judges also need information on alternatives to incarceration and training for use in the preparation of individual sentencing plans. Training programs for judges should include information on mental health and substance abuse issues, including explanations of the appropriateness and availability of various treatment options.

ALTERNATIVES TO INCARCERATION

Contrary to popular opinion (often wrongly informed by politicians and others seeking to appear "tough on crime"), the concept of alternatives to incarceration is not a new one in the criminal justice system. Probation as an alternative to prison has been a component of the system for well over one hundred years. Other alternatives include determination of guilt without further penalty, fine, community service, day reporting, mediation, restitution and electronic monitoring.

In the past twenty years, a broader range of alternatives to incarceration has been developed throughout the country in response to questions about the effectiveness of imprisonment

in decreasing crime, concerns about increasing prison overcrowding, and frustration with the growing costs of building
and operating prisons. Proponents of these alternatives find
themselves challenged to convince the public that prisons are
not the sole response to crime, and that other alternatives can
answer the need for community safety.

Pre-trial release programs provide a pre-trial option for
defendants unable to pay bail costs. These programs alleviate
the portion of jail overcrowding which is due solely to high
numbers of indigent defendants. Pre-trial release supervision
answers both the community's concerns for public safety and
the needs of the defendant for services. These programs
emphasize frequent contact between agency staff and individual defendants, referrals to needed community services, and
monitoring of defendants' court appearances. Costs are sub-
stantially less than the cost of incarcerating the defendant for
two to three months.[21]

Diverting cases to a mediation program is another alternative for removing some cases from the formal court system
before the trial stage. For example, the Court Mediation
Program of the Crime and Justice Foundation in Boston
arranges voluntary mediation between all parties to a crime. At
a cost of $127 per client, the program helps victim and offender
to resolve criminal charges through restitution (repayment of
damages), community service and other arrangements devised
in mediation sessions.[22]

Probation

For those cases that do proceed through the courts, the
most common sentence is probation.[23] Under the terms of a
probationary sentence, an individual is allowed to remain in the

community under supervision of the court or a probation agency of local or state government. Just as incarceration rates have risen dramatically, so have probationary sentences. Today's rate of probation is more than eight times what it was 20 years ago.[24]

Despite the importance of probation within the criminal justice system, most probation departments and agencies are underfunded. Probation officers are faced with overwhelming caseloads, inadequate pay, and lack of community support. Where creative programs exist to work with offenders in the community, these programs generally are too small for the number of prisoners who need them and are viewed as experimental. Lacking the full support of the system, these programs fight ongoing battles for legitimacy, funding and necessary resources.

Probation programs are generally tailored to the individual and can include high or low intensity supervision. Some jurisdictions offer special probation programs for persons who are mentally retarded or who suffer from psychiatric or mental health problems. In many jurisdictions, there are clear racial distinctions that determine which convicted individuals tend to receive probation or other alternatives and which individuals are incarcerated. For example, in New York, more African American men are in prison for felonies than on felony probation whereas white men are on felony probation at three times their rate of incarceration.[25] Many judges are reluctant to sentence whites to "hard time" at state prisons, particularly whites who are convicted of "white collar" crimes. Also, many whites have access to private resources for in-patient drug treatment that are not available to most persons of color.

Electronic Monitoring

In recent years, electronic monitoring has emerged as a popular alternative to incarceration. This option, also known as "electronic tagging," "electronic bracelets" and "electronic home detention," offers a technological solution to the supervision of convicted persons in a community setting. The benefits of this system are that convicted persons wearing the monitors can remain at home, continue to work, maintain family relationships and obtain ready access to community educational and counseling resources. The system replaces the human contact of probation with the electronic guarantee that "tagged" persons are in compliance with the rules of their confinement.

Civil liberties organizations have expressed deep concern about possible abuses of "hi-tech" surveillance devices in people's homes.[26] They argue that adequate funding of probation programs and creative additions to probation programming, such as Intensive Supervised Probation (which provides increased contact between probation officer and client), would serve the same function as electronic monitors. Furthermore, such electronic monitoring systems have high start-up costs which include setting up programs and purchasing equipment such as the bracelets or wrist cuffs worn by offenders, the modems and field monitoring devices installed in the offenders' homes, and the central monitoring unit and host computer.

To address the lack of individual supervision and support provided by standard probation, some jurisdictions have implemented day reporting programs. These transitional programs allow convicted persons to live at home but report to the program center daily. Individuals are required to maintain a job, have a detailed daily schedule, and be closely monitored by program staff.[27]

Restitution and Customer Service

Restitution is a fairly recent innovation for the modern criminal justice system, having been introduced in the mid-1960s.[28] However, the idea of having persons who had committed crimes against individuals and society make amends for those crimes through some form of compensation was common in many ancient societies and cultures. At its core, restitution is designed to begin a healing process that can help both the victim and the convicted person to reorder their lives.

Often restitution is negotiated as a condition of probation. Persons pay restitution in lieu of going to prison or jail. In some instances, individuals who are willing to pay restitution to a victim can avoid a trial altogether through a process that permits criminal charges to be dropped. Unfortunately for individuals who are unemployed or who have erratic work histories, the opportunities to earn the money necessary to pay restitution may not be readily available. Furthermore, in some instances, restitution funds raised from fines and sales of property belonging to convicted persons can cause financial distress to the prisoner's family—individuals who did not commit any crime.

Alternative sentencing plans and restitution agreements sometimes require that, in lieu of incarceration, the offender pay a fine. To avoid the problems incurred by the levying of unreasonable fines, the amount of fines should be based on the offender's ability to pay, generally determined by a combination of the offender's daily income and the seriousness of the offense.

Most community service programs require convicted

persons to perform a set number of hours of volunteer work as a way of "giving back" to the community they harmed. In some jurisdictions, prisoners volunteer to meet with or write to young people as a way of discouraging them from becoming involved in criminal activities. While community service projects tend to be used more often as an alternative to incarceration for white-collar and middle-class convicted persons, opportunities must be developed that allow as many prisoners as possible to participate in community-service projects. As with financial restitution payments, active involvement by prisoners in community service programs can help to alleviate feelings of guilt, worthlessness and resignation.

As initially conceived, probation and other alternatives to incarceration were designed to decrease the number of individuals incarcerated. Instead, the development of alternatives to incarceration has encouraged many judges to place persons who would otherwise be lectured and fined under some sort of restrictive sentence. These programs have not been used as alternatives, but as ad-ons. The unfortunate result is that the total number of persons within the "net" of the criminal justice system has increased dramatically.[29]

PRISONS AND JAILS
The United States imprisons its citizens at a higher rate than any country in the world. Of every 100,000 people in this country, 426 are in prison or jail.[30] Yet, within this total, there are more persons of color imprisoned than whites, with more poor people imprisoned than those from the middle and upper classes.

Unlike most other countries, which have unitary prison systems, there are several types of prisons in the United States.

The basic divisions are among county jails, state prisons and federal prisons; among minimum, medium and maximum security institutions; and between adult and juvenile institutions. However, even within these broad categories, there are many variations. Most prisons are run by government agencies but some, particularly juvenile facilities, are contracted out to private firms and agencies. Most prisons are single-sex, but some are co-educational. Visiting policies and procedures, access to treatment and educational programs, and work leave opportunities all vary from jurisdiction to jurisdiction. Prisons do not even share the same nomenclature; they are "correctional institutions," "penitentiaries," "training schools" or "camps." The result is that there is no easy way to implement system-wide changes.

The statistics that describe prisons in the United States are staggering:

- $13 billion is spent on federal and state prisons local jails each year;
- Per capita spending on prisons and jails has increased by 218 percent during the last decade;
- The average cost to incarcerate one prisoner for 30 years is more than $1 million;
- Interest on bonds used to finance prison construction will reach $600 million by 1995;
- The official crime rate has risen 7.3 percent in the last decade in comparison to a 100 percent increase in the number of people incarcerated;
- 3.5 million men, women and children are under some kind of criminal justice system sanctions or control—incarceration, parole or probation—on any given day.[31]

Since 1980, the federal prisons, the District of Columbia and 18 states have doubled their prison populations. Four states have had threefold increases during the same time period. In 1988, this growth translated into the need for an additional 800 beds per week.[32]

Yet despite the huge expenditures for law enforcement, construction and maintenance, prison conditions in the United States are abysmal. Court orders to improve prison conditions are in effect in 43 United States jurisdictions (including 40 states, Puerto Rico, United States Virgin Islands and the District of Columbia).[33] Prison systems throughout the country are vastly overcrowded, with populations up to 170 percent of capacity.[34] It is common for prisoners to have no assigned beds, sleeping in boiler rooms, gyms or hallways. Basic necessities, including food, health care and physical activity, often are inadequate.

There is a public perception that persons in prison deserve inhumane treatment because they have committed violent acts against others. Even allowing for the assumption that any human being deserves inhumane treatment, the facts do not support that perception because most of those in prison have not been convicted of violent crimes.

Due process often does not exist within prison walls. Disciplinary and grievance procedures in prison are often unfair and unbalanced. Because these proceedings are confidential, prisoners have diminished rights of counsel and appeal. In some prison systems, even though appeal rights are included in official regulations, prisoners have little to no success in actually using those appeal rights. Yet, the prison disciplinary record can be used to prevent release on parole for a prisoner who is otherwise qualified for such release.[35]

The secrecy that is built into the operation of prisons does not allow the public or friends, family members and counselors of prisoners the opportunity to see what is really going on behind prison walls. Often the only time that serious problems are unearthed is when rebellious actions of prisoners cause the media to become involved in covering a prison story.

Most prisons are isolated islands of conflict located in rural regions, too often staffed by Whites and populated by Blacks and other people of color—each in perpetual conflict with the other. Battles often take on an ethnic and class character. Discrimination is rampant within prisons. Persons of color often receive the worst housing assignments, the lowest status jobs and the most severe disciplinary actions. Violence is commonplace—among prisoners and between prisoners and staff. From former prison guards, the Commission learned of the violence inside prisons, especially maximum security prisons. Both former staff and former prisoners told the Commission that brutality by prison guards is permitted and sanctioned. Guards or other staff who try to intervene when colleagues resort to violence are ostracized or threatened.[36]

Prison staffs suffer the effects of working in a highly stressful environment. One estimate holds that many correctional officers die before the age of 54, most often from heart attacks or other stress-induced illness.[37] The high burn-out rates of prison staff are due, in part, to overcrowded prison conditions with prisoners who are culturally different, younger, frustrated and angry at the forced idleness and hopelessness of their situation. Guards and other staff often feel unappreciated and looked down upon by the same society that demands that more and more people be locked up.

The stress on control has led to placing convicted persons under more stringent security arrangements than is necessary to maintain order. There is a clear trend toward more extensive use of high security prisons, including "supermaxes," "control units" and overclassification of prisoners.* The existence of the Marion Penitentiary and similar facilities on the federal level has led to a burst of construction of similar facilities on the state level. These new high-tech facilities are purportedly built for prisoners who are uncontrollably violent. In many jurisdictions, however, prisoners who pose no major risk of violence or escape are held in high security units for long periods of time and denied services or programs available elsewhere in the prison or the prison system.[38]

Boot Camps

In recent years, there has been increasing emphasis on military-style boot camps (also known as shock incarceration camps) as an incarceration option, particularly for young adults. Although sometimes referred to as an alternative to incarceration, boot camps are, in fact, another form of prison. These boot camps emphasize rigorous physical training, complete submission to authority and severely regimented behavior. Because prisoners generally choose to enter these programs (albeit with only one other option—a much longer sentence in a standard jail or prison), the programs also appear fairer than standard sentencing practices.

Boot camps are more attractive than prisons to many

* Long-term solitary confinement in a prison is not appropriate even for so-called "uncontrollably violent" persons. Programs should be designed which work to address the causes (including psychological causes) of prolonged, repeated violent behavior.

convicted persons because the camps are an alternative to overcrowded prisons and are generally short-term in duration. The camps are attractive to judges because they emphasize harsh punishment as a way to "teach prisoners a lesson" and are, therefore, in line with current calls for "toughness." While long-term success or failure of boot camps has not been shown, it is clear that these programs fail to address the real needs of offenders for education, counseling, drug treatment or job training. Instead, the camps appear to offer an easy, quick answer to a difficult and complicated problem. While boot camps do develop a sense of unity among program participants, these programs serve to reduce, rather than strengthen, prisoners' individual ability to analyze situations and make personal life choices. Perhaps most troubling is their emphasis upon physical public humiliation, violence and the rigid militarism of the armed service basic training programs after which they are designed.

Prison Reform

Efforts to improve prison conditions are often met with hostility by prison staff, whether those efforts are championed by prisoners themselves or by advocates from the outside. Prisoners who speak out for better conditions often find themselves facing strong sanctions by the prison administration and by individual guards. (This is particularly true if they have filed law suits against the prison administration.) Prison staff and administrators believe prisoner activism is a hindrance to the smooth running of prisons. There is little structural opportunity for prisoners and administrators to work together to solve problems in the institution. Lack of trust between the groups, the dynamics of control held by the staff, the constant atmosphere of violence, and the barriers to family and community involvement all serve as obstacles to cooperative problem solving. The situation is made worse by the overcrowding and overdependence on high-level incarceration.

Individuals from the outside are disparaged by prison officials as "bleeding hearts" and "do-gooders" or "revolutionaries" and "trouble-makers," depending on their political orientation, religious affiliation or personal style. Prison officials generally oppose what they see as unnecessary meddling. Individuals with prior prison records who have been released and who may be quite knowledgeable about prison conditions are usually rejected out-of-hand as prison advocates because their presence is alleged to be inflammatory to guards and prisoners.

Yet, the opposition to advocates of prison reform from within and outside the walls does not mean that all prison administrators are satisfied with the status quo. Many of those who work in the prison system are frustrated by the lack of adequate funding, attacks from the public for stricter prison systems and demands from prisoner advocates for fewer restrictions. Criminal justice professionals who work to develop more humane prison systems and alternatives to incarceration face criticism from both colleagues and the general public.

PAROLE AND POST-RELEASE

More than 95 percent of all persons who go to jail or prison ultimately are released back into the community.[39] The federal prison system has eliminated parole altogether but provides for a term of supervised release after full completion of the prison term. In state and county prison systems, convicted persons who are sentenced to jail or prison are released from the institution either at the completion of the sentence or on parole. Individuals who "max out" (complete their sentences) are released without supervision while those on parole are "conditionally" released with supervision continuing until the completion of the sentence.

Since each of the separate states operates its own criminal justice system, laws, regulations and procedures, policies and practices regarding release differ from jurisdiction to jurisdiction. For example, some states utilize indeterminate sentencing in which persons can be paroled at any point, while others use determinate sentencing which specifies a minimum and a maximum amount of time to be served. Most states provide opportunities for parole except for persons facing execution or, in a few states, those jailed for life without possibility of parole.

Parole Systems

In most jurisdictions, parole is not automatic but must be granted by a Parole Board or similar entity. As with other bodies within the criminal justice system, these Boards are often infused with racism and subject to societal pressures to be "tough on crime" and "tougher on criminals." While the composition of these Boards varies from state to state, most are overwhelmingly white.

The parole system is often attacked as a means of coddling criminals, yet, its function is to provide a supervised transition of prisoners back into the community rather than an abrupt release at the end of the sentence with no supports. Also, parole reduces prison overcrowding, is less costly and serves as a tangible prize for good behavior while in prison. However, as part of the parole process, a prisoner usually must show a parole plan which includes employment and a place to live. For many persons of color, those supports are not available.

As with probation and alternatives to incarceration, parole and post-release programs are underfunded. Staff face problems of impossible caseloads, inadequate resources and lack of appreciation for their work. Some go beyond the requirements of their jobs in trying to help ex-prisoners find jobs and housing after release; this extra work is often without recompense or recognition. Other parole officers burn out, become cynical and find themselves going through the motions, unable to continue caring about their clients. Parole staff are further hampered by lack of adequate service resources in the community. For example, faced with clients needing drug counseling, often the best they can do is to get them on months-long waiting lists.

Another key issue for parole staff is the racism within the system. Speaking anonymously to state officials, a spokesperson for a group of African American parole agents in the Philadelphia area identified a pattern of discrimination in which African American parole officers were "written up" for minor infractions that were ignored when committed by Whites. These negative entries in the personnel records of the officers made it virtually impossible for African Americans to rise to administrative positions. "Sometimes it seems that Whites cannot make the distinction between clients and staff," he said. "They just see a Black face whether its a parolee or a co-worker and think that there's got to be a problem somewhere."[40]

At the community level, family and friends often become exhausted from supporting ex-prisoners who need access to service programs that either do not exist or are overloaded. This is particularly true of ex-prisoners who are also drug or alcohol addicts, or who have no experience in holding a steady job or maintaining a household.

One element that the Commission believes should be included as part of parole and release arrangements is restitution. One of the drawbacks of restitution (as it is currently used in most jurisdictions) is that it is not available to individuals who are incarcerated because most persons in jail have little or no money with which to pay debts of any kind. If prisoners were paid fair wages for their work in various prison industries, it would be possible for incarcerated men and women to participate in restitution programs also and thereby begin in this way to confront the true nature of their crime or crimes and the impact on others.

Parole Violations

Parole policies are designed to insure that prisoners do not commit further crimes and return to prison. Yet, these same policies often increase the likelihood of recidivism. Persons on parole are often forbidden contact with associates in their home communities, making maintenance of family and cultural ties more difficult. Violations of parole regulations, even those which are not violations of criminal law, can send a convicted person back to prison. Among the technical parole violations that are not crimes are curfew violation, being in the wrong part of town, marrying without permission, leaving town for a few days without getting approval, having a beer, missing appointments at out-patient therapy programs or failing to report to the parole agent.

Lack of adequate job training and job placement programs, educational programs, medical care and housing for ex-prisoners compound the difficulties. The pressures ex-prisoners face, both emotional and financial, upon release from prison

are exacerbated by society's tendency to view persons who
have served time in prison or jail as permanently damaged and
unredeemable.

Technical parole violations have contributed substan-
tially to prison overcrowding as paroled prisoners return to
incarceration due to parole violations. Nationally, one out of
five incarcerated persons is in prison for a technical parole
violation.

Whether released on parole or at the end of a sentence, ex-
prisoners face serious difficulties in reintegrating back into the
community. Many women and men leave prison full of hopes
for a successful life in the community, only to end up disillu-
sioned and alienated. The Commission heard testimony from
ex-prisoners who spoke of being forced to either lie about
having a prison record or telling the truth and being refused
employment or housing. Individuals who obtained high school
diplomas and college degrees while incarcerated found themselves unemployable and unwanted.[41] The stigma of having
been in prison is strong enough to cost ex-prisoners jobs,
housing, family relationships, friendships and needed community support. As a result, many give up the struggle to succeed
honestly and return to survival strategies that are often dangerous, harmful, violent and illegal.

CAPITAL PUNISHMENT

The United States is one of few modern industrialized
nations that continues the practice of state-sanctioned killing.
Executions in the United States have been the target of protest
and outrage from international human rights organizations,
including Amnesty International. Exacerbated by the current
War on Drugs and its calls for execution of drug dealers, the

trend in criminal justice legislation and policy in the United States is to increase the use of the death penalty, and to increase the number of offenses for which a sentence of death is imposed. Capital punishment in the United States has a particular impact upon people of color, since African Americans and Native Americans are greatly overrepresented on the death rows of this country.

The Commission opposes capital punishment for the following reasons:

1. Execution is killing and is, therefore, morally wrong.
2. The death penalty restores no one to life. Victims of crime and family members of murder victims often believe they should seek a death sentence for the person who has killed their loved one. They are led by prosecutors and politicians to believe that once the execution is carried out, justice will have been served, and their troubles will be over. In fact, the needs of victims and survivors for counseling, health care and financial assistance are not met by a death sentence, which only creates another violent act with which the victim and survivor must cope.[42]
3. The death penalty does not deter crime. In fact, states which impose the death penalty for murder have been shown to have higher murder rates. [43]
4. The death penalty is racist. The race of the defendant and, especially, the race of the victim, strongly influence who is chosen to be executed in the United States.[44] When African Americans are killed, the criminal justice system does not give high priority to the crime, but when a white person is killed, especially by a Black person, the crime is treated with the highest priority and vigor.

The Commission believes use of the death penalty, for any reason, must be ended. Creative, broad public education must be conducted to insure that the myths about the death penalty do not continue to thrive. Churches, schools, legislative bodies and community organizations must engage in organizing efforts to end capital punishment.

IV
IMPACT OF DRUGS

There is probably no single element that has had more impact on the criminal justice system in recent years than the influx of drugs—particularly crack-cocaine. The criminal justice system's response has been to focus primarily on underclass and immigrant populations. Open-air drug markets and crack houses in low-income neighborhoods have served as a flashpoint, encouraging vigilantism and serious internal divisions within communities of color on how drugs should be stopped. For the most part, the answer has been simplistic: more jail cells and longer prison terms.

Yet, the severity of sentences for drug sales and use has not made the problem go away. The amount of money that can be made in the crack and cocaine market is so substantial that drug kingpins have no difficulty recruiting new employees to replace those who leave the operations—generally as a result of incarceration or death. The trend for longer sentences has had one major impact. Adolescents and pre-adolescents (some of whom are not even drug users) increasingly are being recruited into street-level drug organizations. The reason for this "youth" orientation is that juvenile criminal justice systems are generally less punitive for drug-related crimes than adult systems.

Increased public calls for harsh punishment have resulted in new mandatory sentences for many drug-related crimes, filling the prisons with substance abusers. Prisons are seen as the answer to the drug crisis because many people truly believe that incarceration gets drug dealers and users off the streets and away from drugs. While prisons and jails do take drug users away from the immediate neighborhood temporarily, it does not necessarily take them away from drugs. In fact, as prisoners can attest, drugs and alcohol often are as available in prisons and jails as in the community. Guards and other prison staff are frequently responsible for bringing drugs into the institutions, where the drugs are used as bargaining chips and as a means of control. Little attention has been given to the greater effectiveness and lower cost of treating addicts outside of prison. According to a recent study, for every drug offender sentenced to prison, three offenders could be treated in an inpatient treatment program and 16 in an outpatient program.[45]

A recent study sponsored by the National Institute of Justice showed that more than 70 percent of all men and women arrested in the cities of San Diego, New York, Philadelphia and Chicago tested positive for one or more drugs. This represented persons arrested for non-drug related crimes as well as drug-related ones.[46] For most of these individuals, drug use is not just a bad habit, it is an addiction. Therefore, without treatment, it is unlikely that many of these persons will be able to give up their drug of "choice."

If prisons and jails had well-designed and effective intensive drug treatment programs, a case could be made that incarcerating drug users is a way of getting individuals off drugs. However, in this regard, prisons and jails parallel the community: there are few treatment programs for low-income individuals and persons of color, but there are long waiting lists for entry. Where programs do exist, including some that are highly successful, they are able to handle only a small fraction of the addicted prison population. The lack of treatment facilities is especially critical for adolescents and women, particularly women who are pregnant or who have dependent children.

The public perception is that most drug dealers and users are African American, Latino or Asian. The reason for this perception is clear—mass media tends to concentrate coverage on sensationalized drug busts in the inner cities and dramatic interdiction efforts geared at Jamaicans, Cubans and South East Asians. Yet, the actual complexion of the drug trade and drug use in this country is primarily White. Federal surveys show that 69 percent of all cocaine users in the United States are White and that two-thirds of all drug users hold regular jobs.[47]

Imprisonment for drug use is highly selective. In New York State, for example, Whites are three times more likely than non-Whites to be on felony probation. Whites constitute approximately 30 percent of the arrests for sale and possession of drugs in New York but represented less than 10 percent of the commitments to state prisons in 1988 for drug-related crimes. Even though most drug users in the state are White, 90 percent of the people in New York state prisons for drugs are African American.[48] This pattern is repeated across the country.

In testimony before the National Commission for Crime and Justice, Jim Murphy, Director of the New York State

Coalition for Criminal Justice noted:

> Judging by state imprisonment, it is not too far-
> fetched to say that the state has effectively legalized
> drugs for Whites. The "War on Drugs" is having
> much better success in arresting and imprisoning
> street dealers in poor and mainly minority
> communities than getting major dealers or the
> users who drive the business.[49]

It is clear that this society's approach to drug use has been
to treat it as a crime rather than as an illness. Yet, with this
punitive approach, the problem has only worsened. Resources
that could easily have been directed toward establishing community-based drug treatment centers, more and better ways of
treating addictions, and employment alternatives for young
people who work in the drug trade have gone instead toward
building more prisons and hiring more prison guards and police
officers. It is imperative that the focus be shifted away from
punishment and incarceration and toward a deeper understanding of why so many persons in the United States feel the need
to take such risks to escape into oblivion.

The Commission believes that community-based programs should be established that are specifically designed to
treat persons addicted to drugs and that these programs should
be replicated across the nation. In instances where persons with
drug problems are incarcerated, treatment should be provided
for every prisoner who requests it. Drug treatment programs
should be designed in a holistic manner with special attention
to culture, identity, gender, age and life experiences. Peer-led
support groups should be developed to help individuals deal
with their difficulties in ways other than getting high on drugs.

V

SPECIAL POPULATIONS

The prison population in the United States is actually comprised of many different segments of society, each with special characteristics and special needs. Prisons take note of some general differences, such as establishing separate facilities for juveniles and women. In other cases, such as immigrants and refugees or individuals who are not fluent in English, support systems are lacking. The Commission has identified a series of special populations for which additional programming and services are needed in order to ensure justice: juveniles, women, refugees, immigrants and non-English speaking persons. Furthermore, specific discriminatory patterns directed against political prisoners and prisoners with AIDS were identified. These practices constitute denial of their equal rights, in clear violation of international laws and generally accepted standards of human decency.

JUVENILES

The criminal justice system in the United States is divided into adult and juvenile divisions, with age being the determining factor. As a rule, age is the major factor in determining where a convicted person is placed. While adults in most systems are persons at least 18 years old, in some situations, juveniles who commit so-called "adult" crimes are sentenced to adult prisons. In some instances, adolescents convicted of murder and rape have been sent to maximum security adult institutions. Young people who have been convicted of serious crimes may be kept in juvenile institutions until they reach age 18 and then are transferred to adult prisons. The United States is also one of only a few nations in the world that sentences juveniles to death.

Juvenile facilities are distinguished from adult facilities in that they allow young people the opportunity to become rehabilitated without having a permanent criminal record. As a result, many states to do not allow the names of youthful prisoners to be made public; they expunge the juvenile criminal records of individuals when they reach 18 years of age.

Facilities designed for juveniles often are called "training schools," "camps" or even "study centers." There are approximately 600,000 admissions to juvenile detention facilities annually, with over 50,000 adolescents confined on any given day.[50] Of those youth who are incarcerated in juvenile facilities, the majority are persons of color. African American and Latino youth, particularly males, run extremely high risks of being stopped and/or arrested in "sweeps."*

---

* A "sweep" is a police operation in which a large number of individuals are rounded up as suspects, often based on extremely general suspect profiles.

Many young people are arrested and convicted for economic crimes. There are also widespread incidences of violent behavior by youth. It is estimated that 60 percent of the juveniles in custody use illegal drugs.[51] Despite this, few drug treatment programs satisfactorily address the specific problems of adolescents, particularly those from communities of color.

Much of the crime in inner-city communities is committed by youth who are members of gangs. The media often stereotype these young people as "subhuman," "animals" and "wolf-packs"; they are thought to lack redeeming qualities. Many community anti-crime activists, horrified by the level of violence brought into the neighborhood by these gangs, believe that these young people should be written off as a lost generation and that the focus should be placed on younger children to prevent them from becoming lost as well. The danger in this approach is that program services are being withheld from the young people already caught up in the criminal justice system. Many of these youth have great potential but need to channel their talents in more productive directions.

It is clear that the existing juvenile justice system has not been effective in deflecting disadvantaged youth from criminal behavior. The Commission believes that one reason for this is that there has to be active and continuous involvement of communities of color in programs for children and youth. Efforts to establish programs in communities of color for youths who have been convicted of crimes often meet serious and sustained resistance from local residents who are fearful of increased crime and gang violence.[52] Yet, without strong support from communities for these young people, prospects for future incarceration as adults remain intolerably high.

WOMEN

For most of this nation's history, women prisoners have been a rarity. That is changing. In 1980, there were approximately 13,000 women in federal and state prisons. By the end of 1989, that number had more than tripled to nearly 41,000. Although women represent only about six percent of the entire prison population, the number of female prisoners is growing at a rate of 15 percent annually, almost twice the rate of increase in men's incarceration.[53] The overrepresentation of women of color in prison is even more dramatic than that of men. For example, in some jurisdictions, African American and Latino women comprise over 70 percent of the prison and jail populations of women.[54]

There are many reasons for this increase. Some of the change is undoubtedly due to a spill-over of the nation's efforts to equalize conditions for men and women. Thus, women not only have greater access to jobs that were designated for men, they also have greater access to punishments that were similarly designed. Another important element is increased use of illegal drugs by women, particularly crack-cocaine. As early as 1979, it was estimated that between 50 and 60 percent of incarcerated women had drug dependency problems. Current estimates indicate an increase to as high as 80 percent.[55]

Historically, few judges were willing to sentence a woman to prison, particularly if she was the custodial parent for dependent children. However, mandatory sentencing requirements, particularly for drug-related and violent crimes, have taken much of the sentencing discretion out of the hands of judges. For example, in some jurisdictions the law has mandated stiff sentences for women who have killed or severely injured abusive spouses. Two governors have recently granted clemency to such women, recognizing from the executive level the extenuating circumstances that judges and juries were not permitted to acknowledge.

Many women are arrested for so-called victimless crimes, such as prostitution. Economic crimes, such as writing bad checks and shoplifting, also are relatively common among incarcerated populations of women. Nearly 75 percent of crimes for which women are imprisoned nationwide can be traced to their socioeconomic conditions.[56] While only a small percentage of women are convicted of violent crime, that number has been rising in recent years.

At Commission hearings in Atlanta, several witnesses testified about the special problems encountered by women in prison. Once a woman is incarcerated, her family (particularly her children) often becomes caught up in the criminal justice system. Eight out of ten female prisoners have children. Of those, 70 percent are single parents, most with sole custody.[57] With imprisonment, ties are often severed between parent and child, with the child being placed in foster care or a group home situation. Because of the stigma that society places on "fallen women," families of incarcerated women tend to be far less supportive than families of incarcerated men. Additionally, women are more likely to have a spouse or significant other who is also caught up in the justice system. The result is that incarcerated women are often terribly isolated, with few links to the community.

Some prison systems have addressed the problem by providing education and job training, particularly in non-traditional fields that often provide better earning potential than jobs that have traditionally been filled by women. These programs also have helped women to gain skills in child rearing that they can use when they are released and reunited with their children.

REFUGEES AND IMMIGRANTS

People who come to the United States without officially recognized entry documents are often introduced immediately to the criminal justice system. Conditions of detention for persons seeking asylum in the United States frequently are horrendous. Amnesty International reports that United States Immigration and Nationalization officials often detain refugees as a way of deterring others from seeking refuge in this country.[58] Such actions are in violation of international law, which stipulates that detention be used only when absolutely necessary and which places the burden of proof of that necessity upon the government.

Many of the detention centers, particularly those on the United States-Mexico border, are designed to warehouse individuals. Entire families are housed in facilities where their space is marked by tape on the floor. In some instances, refugees wear florescent jumpsuits and march to meals in single file.[59] To further demonstrate the restrictive nature of the centers, complexes are sometimes surrounded by fences topped by coils of razor ribbon.

Many of the individuals who are placed in these centers and camps have fled terrible human rights abuses, traveling a long, arduous and often dangerous journey to "freedom." To be treated as criminals is so debilitating that some give up hope and drop their asylum claims, allowing themselves to be deported in spite of the life-threatening risk they may face upon return.[60]

The insistence of relying on incarceration to solve social

problems affects even those coming to the United States to escape injustice in other lands. That nearly all of those detained upon entry are people of color points again to the role of racism in United State imprisonment policy. In the 1980s, refugees from Eastern Europe were far less likely to face imprisonment than were refugees from Haiti, El Salvador or Guatemala.[61]

Refugees who are detained in the United States face a number of serious problems in addition to harsh conditions of confinement. Detainees are often held in areas far from refugee support services. They face rapid and sometimes unannounced transfers from one location to another, causing further difficulty in access to services. Those refugees who do not speak English well often receive inappropriate, misleading and incorrect information regarding legal services and political asylum. Lawsuits have been filed challenging these INS practices. Minors who have committed no crimes are detained in the same facilities as adults charged with criminal offenses. In some instances, potential asylum seekers are detained in facilities such as county jails, where access to assistance in claiming asylum is severely limited.

For immigrants who have not been detained but who do not have legal status, any interaction with the criminal justice system is used as grounds for deportation. Often efforts are made to eject them from the United States prior to a trial to determine guilt or innocence of charges. In California, legislation was introduced recently that would have allowed all persons without proper documentation who are arrested but not charged to be summarily referred to the INS for deportation.[62]

In many instances, immigrants are unfairly branded as drug smugglers. This is particularly true for those from South America, parts of Southeast Asia, the Caribbean and Mexico.

Thus, the War on Drugs provides police and prosecutors with the excuse to the abrogate legal rights of the individuals, especially on the United States-Mexico border. This is particularly true for persons who are unfamiliar with the structure of the American legal system and/or lack fluency in English. Citizens who fit the stereotypical description of an "immigrant" are likely to face discrimination and ill treatment in their interactions with the criminal justice system.

In the particular case of Puerto Ricans, in which citizenship was decreed by the United States Congress in 1917, the same problems exist; although Puerto Ricans are citizens, they may be unfamiliar with the mainland legal system, may not speak English and are not seen by the general public as Americans.[63]

The result is that a dichotomy has been established whereby due process is reserved for "Americans" (particularly white Americans). All others (including the foreign-born and American persons of color) must suffer under a system that basically characterizes individuals as guilty unless they can prove otherwise.

NON-ENGLISH SPEAKING PERSONS

Prisoners who are not fluent in English face special problems. In most jurisdictions, there are few bilingual and bicultural staff. Prisoners who speak in their native languages are punished. Men and women who do not speak English well are often denied access to counseling, job training and educational programs because those programs are offered by staff that is English-speaking only. In some instances, even prison guards and other staff who speak Spanish or other languages are not allowed to converse with prisoners in anything other than English.

To address language issues, some prisons hire persons who have rudimentary knowledge of a second language. However, poor translations can cause additional problems. Those who are bilingual but not bicultural sometimes lack sufficient understanding of the nuances of culture, tradition and history.

The United States is becoming more of a pluralist society. A recent study by the policy research group, California Tomorrow, noted that non-whites will soon be the majority in California. This country cannot, therefore, continue to see itself as having only one language or one culture. Services in the community and in the criminal justice system must reflect the reality of the multilingual, multicultural society that exists in the United States.

Given the increasing numbers of incarcerated persons for whom English is not their primary language, the Commission believes it is crucial that communications in various languages become part of criminal justice policies. This can be accomplished by hiring skilled bilingual staff and providing accurate translations of oral and written materials and instructions.

POLITICAL PRISONERS

Officially the United States does not recognize the existence of political prisoners within its borders.* Yet, the Interfaith Prisoners of Conscience Project of the National Council of Churches estimates that there are more than 100 political prisoners in United States prisons.[64] The Special International

---

* Many other countries have a legally recognized category of political prisoners, with certain rights.

Tribunal on the Violation of Human Rights of Political Prisoners and Prisoners of War in United States Prisons and Jails, which was convened in New York in December, 1990, identified as United States political prisoners "persons incarcerated for actions carried out in support of legitimate struggles for self-determination or for opposing the illegal policies of the United States government and/or its political sub-divisions." According to testimony provided to the Tribunal, political prisoners in this country have received "draconian disproportionate sentences and have been subjected to torture, as well as cruel, discriminatory and degrading punishment.[65]

Political prisoners in the United States are generally held under much harsher conditions than other prisoners: locked in cells for up to 23 hours a day, denied contact with family and friends and denied adequate health treatment.[66] Political prisoners often are held in special high security prisons or transferred frequently and without notice, making access to lawyers and maintenance of family ties extremely difficult. The secrecy surrounding political prisoners decreases the opportunities for community support for these prisoners and their families.

The treatment of these prisoners, many of whom represent self-determination movements of Puerto Ricans, Native Americans and African Americans, is not justified by the facts of the cases. As was determined in a recent court decision:

> It is one thing to place persons under greater security because they have escape histories and pose special risks to our correctional institutions. But consigning anyone to a high security unit for past political associations they will never shed unless forced to renounce them is a dangerous mission for this country's prison system to continue.
> Baraldini v. Meese, 691 F. Supp. (1988)

Evidence indicates that the United States government metes out the longest sentences of any country in the world to its political prisoners.[67] Most political prisoners and prisoners of war are serving the equivalent of natural life in prison. For example, Puerto Rican political prisoners have sentences that average 67 years.[68]

The Commission feels strongly that the United States must recognize the existence of political prisoners and respect and comply with the Standard Minimum Rules for the Treatment of Prisoners established by the United Nations and monitored by the United Nations and Amnesty International.

PRISONERS WITH AIDS

In recent years, AIDS has posed an additional dilemma for the criminal justice system. Prisons provide an ideal environment for the spread of HIV infection, largely because of the high number of incarcerated persons with histories of intravenous drug use and the relative frequency of anonymous and casual sex, including male homosexual activities.

The situation will undoubtedly get much worse. Projections are that the percentage of drug users in United States prisons and jails will rise from the current rate of just under 50 percent to 70 percent by 1995.[69] According to the National Commission on AIDS, "the national policy of mandatory sentencing for drug offenders (who have very high rates of HIV infection) has placed an enormous strain on weak prison health care systems."[70]

Most prisons and jails are not equipped to handle persons with AIDS. The institutions have neither the facilities nor the staff to provide the sophisticated and intensive nursing care and psychosocial support services required. Rather than try to modify the prison health system to address this crisis, the Commission believes that it is far more constructive to release nonviolent persons with HIV infection and AIDS into the community where their illnesses can be treated in hospitals, hospices and family residences with nursing care. This type of early release can save states money, since Medicaid picks up a substantial portion of the medical costs for persons who are released to community settings.

Because AIDS is an incurable, although increasingly treatable disease, education and prevention efforts are key. Misinformation about HIV infection and AIDS is common among prisoners, families of prisoners and institutional staff, including guards. Community-based health and human service organizations and volunteers offering AIDS education and counseling often find access to prisoners and staff extremely difficult. In some cases, access is blocked altogether.

As a result of poor information flow, many guards are reluctant to work with persons who have HIV infection. A 1988 Survey of Federal Bureau of Corrections staff found that 40 percent were "bothered a great deal" by the presence of HIV positive inmates and 14 percent considered leaving their jobs.[71] Similarly, many prisoners are reluctant to share living space with infected individuals. Effective AIDS education can defuse potentially violent situations and assist in facilitating housing arrangements.

The most important role for AIDS education is to stem the spread of the infection and disease. While many educational models have been tried within prisons and jails to change prisoner behavior, it appears that the most effective ones have utilized peer educators—incarcerated men and women who have been trained and certified to provide AIDS education. These peer educators are effective because they speak the same language as the prisoners, are more aware of specific risk behaviors in the prison and are on-site and readily available.[72] They can provide information and promote compassionate behavior for those with HIV infection and AIDS. Some prison systems have experimented with distribution of condoms to prison populations as part of a broader educational campaign regarding means of transmission and ways to minimize risk.

Counseling is also important, particularly in environments where testing for HIV infection takes place. Mandatory testing is particularly problematic without the informed consent of individuals and when accompanied by little or no counseling. Such testing simply serves to stigmatize the prisoner, often with no additional access to health services that could prolong life.

Persons with HIV infection face discrimination in many criminal justice systems. As of 1991, 16 state prisons segregate all prisoners diagnosed with AIDS, five segregate those who are HIV positive and symptomatic but have not developed full-blown AIDS, and four segregate everyone who has been found to be infected with HIV, whether symptomatic or not.[73]

According to the 1991 National Commission on AIDS Report, "segregation clearly identifies the infected in a prison population, literally labeling these individuals and rendering them at greater risk for assaults, discrimination and disparate treatment." Placing persons with HIV infection or AIDS in a designated location violates a prisoner's right to privacy, for such actions expose their health to other prisoners and guards. Infected persons often lose access to religious services, work programs, visitation rights, libraries (including law libraries), educational and recreational programs and drug and alcohol treatment. Isolation of prisoners can lead to severe depression, with AIDS units becoming a kind of "Death Row." It is also important to consider that segregating persons with HIV infection lulls the rest of the prison population into a false sense of security (i.e., if the infected persons are removed, everyone else is safe).[74]

Since most prisoners are eventually released, it is important that prisons and jails avoid becoming incubators for HIV infection. Persons with AIDS, who are not a threat to the community, should be allowed early release to environments that are better suited to providing proper medical, psychosocial care and a family support system. Education and prevention efforts should be increased.

VI
SUPPORT PROGRAMS

═══════════

One of the major failings of prisons and jails is that they do not provide necessary service and support to prisoners who are within their walls. Opportunities to provide education, job training, counseling and preventive health care are wasted. The Commission heard testimony on many of these areas at the hearings and has suggestions and recommendations for changes. Prisons and jails are not the best way to deal with most persons who have been convicted of crimes. However, if they are to be used, they should help individuals improve themselves and prepare for productive lives in the communities to which they will return.

EMPLOYMENT

Most of the individuals in America's prisons and jails were previously unemployed or underemployed. The lack of solid work histories for most prisoners is due to a combination of factors: functional illiteracy, few marketable skills, discrimination within the work force and few available jobs.

In light of these factors, the Commission believes that a major task of the nation's prisons and jails should be to prepare prisoners for jobs in the outside world. However, this is not the case in most jurisdictions. Employment programs tend to be viewed by prison administrations as "make work" activities to keep prisoners occupied while they serve their sentences. Persons confined to jails for relatively short periods of time often are deemed ineligible for employment and training programs. Long-term prisoners are frequently placed in routine maintenance jobs so that the prison can have a dependable work force for such positions. Transfers from institution to institution can also short-circuit a prisoner's efforts to obtain more meaningful employment.

The jobs that are offered as part of prison industries (like making license plates) tend to be tasks that are unskilled, non-challenging and have no counterparts outside the prison walls. In many instances, prisons do not have up-to-date, computer-based equipment or instructors who are knowledgeable about the current job market. As a result, the employment experiences of most prisoners do not prepare them for any future employment other than non-skilled, minimum-wage jobs.

Wages paid to prisoners for the work they perform within institutions are extremely low—usually just enough to buy cigarettes or stamps. Yet, despite the low wages, many prisoners will forgo participation in highly beneficial education and training classes and counseling programs for the chance to work at menial prison jobs for a few dollars a day.

The Commission believes that prisoners should be given meaningful work that is appropriately compensated. The funds earned can then be used to help cover the costs of victim restitution and family support and can be placed in escrow accounts for post-release expenses. If prisoners were paid a fair wage, prison industries could compete in the marketplace without objections from other businesses that the low wages paid to prisoners represent unfair competition.

EDUCATION AND TRAINING

Because functional illiteracy is so common among persons who have been convicted of crimes, educational programs are an essential component of prison program services. Yet, it is sometimes difficult to convince adult prisoners to admit to their educational deficiencies. Adult Basic Education (ABE), high school General Equivalency Diploma (GED) classes and English as a Second Language (ESL) can help to equip prisoners with the skills in reading, writing, computing and critical thinking that are required by employers. For many prisoners, completion of one of these basic educational programs is a prerequisite for enrolling in specialized employment skills programs.

The difficulties that teachers face in providing quality educational programs in prisons and jails are formidable. Many prisoners have had negative experiences with schools and, as a result, are hostile toward any type of formal educational environment. Classroom space is often at a premium as institutions become more overcrowded. With the increased emphasis on security, educational programs have become almost superfluous in some institutions. And while there may be a willingness to hire teachers, there is rarely a financial commitment to incorporate the interactive video equipment and micro-computers that would allow structured, self-paced and individualized learning for the prisoner population.

Also, prisoners have few incentives to go to class. Time devoted to lessons may translate into fewer opportunities for recreation and family visits. The connection between education and employment is often unclear, especially when basic skills are taught in isolation and not within the context of vocational and practical situations.[75] The Commission feels that positive self-image, decision-making and other social skills must be woven into the curriculum of prison education programs for these programs to be effective. Material must be presented in a way that recognizes the racial and cultural diversity of the prisoners.

Prison systems should identify areas for skills training that will allow prisoners to actually enter the work force and become gainfully employed when they are released. Training should be provided on up-to-date equipment, using the latest techniques and approaches. In addition, instruction should be offered in ancillary areas such as proper attire for the workplace, filling out application forms, reading manuals and instruction booklets and punctuality. For women, it is important to provide training in non-traditional areas that typically offer higher wages than jobs usually filled by women.

HEALTH CARE

Prisons and jails have been properly described as "backwaters of health care."[76] In 1976, in *Estelle v. Gamble*, the United States Supreme Court interpreted the 8th Amendment's prohibition against "cruel and unusual punishment" to require that "deliberate indifference to serious medical needs of inmates" constitutes a violation of a prisoner's protected rights. As a result, many of the jurisdictions that are currently under court orders to improve conditions have been cited specifically for lack of adequate medical services.[77]

Throughout the nation, communities of color tend to have significantly higher rates of illness and injury thanWhite communities.[78] When individuals from those communities are confined to prisons and jails, the likelihood of health problems increase. Overcrowded prison conditions heighten the spread of infectious diseases. Preventive health care is rarely offered, and when prisoners complain of pain or health-related problems, they are often accused of faking.

Many prisoners have specific health-related problems that are related to drug abuse, alcoholism and prior injuries. The problem of AIDS has placed additional burdens on prison health systems, and tuberculosis is also on the rise. As prison populations age because of longer sentences, prison physicians, nurses and health care workers must address chronic illnesses that are more common in older populations. Health care for women is particularly deficient; in many prisons, women do not receive routine gynecological services, such as detection and treatment of sexually transmitted diseases, pap smears and breast examinations.[79] The Commission believes that health care for prisoners must become a priority in all institutions.

FAMILY LINKAGES

The sheer number of persons of color in prisons and jails has a major impact on family structure within those communities. When an individual is punished through imprisonment, frequently that person's entire family suffers. This is particularly true when women are incarcerated, the majority of whom have custody of their children. However, nearly half of all incarcerated men also have custody of dependent children, usually as part of married relationships.[80]

There are a litany of problems that affect families of prisoners. The initial reactions of family members at time of arrest often include shock and disbelief, followed by guilt, depression, anxiety, anger and fear.[81] Behavior tends to vary according to individual situations and the stability of relationships. Once an individual goes to prison, a new set of problems arise. Although studies have shown that prisoners who maintain-ties with families have lower recidivism rates, the structure of prison life tends to make the maintenance of those ties difficult. The Commission heard repeatedly from families of prisoners and persons working in family programs with prisons about the difficulties.

In many jurisdictions, the proximity of a prison or jail to a prisoner's family is not considered when a prisoner is assigned. Furthermore, since most prisons are located in rural areas, even a "nearby" prison may be located too far away for spouses, children, parents and significant others to visit or call on a regular basis. This is particularly true for low-income families where dependence on public transportation or favors from friends with access to cars can make a frequent visitation schedule impossible. If children are involved, the costs of food, transportation and lodging are compounded.

Yet, even when transportation can be easily arranged and afforded, other circumstances often intervene to keep prisoner families apart. Prisoners often feel guilty about being unable to provide financial and emotional support to family members and, as a result, tend to pull away from ongoing relationships. In many cases, the prisoners turn instead to their "prison family," replacing loved ones at home. The financial deprivation that incarceration of a family breadwinner causes also can strain relationship bonds.

Within prisons and jails, actively fostering family connections is often viewed as an added burden by the institutions. Visitation, as with any form of increased contact between the public and prisoners, can disrupt prison schedules, compromise security and provide opportunities for the introduction of contraband. Guards and prison staff can be quite antagonistic towards family visitors, viewing them as "bad influences" on the convicted persons. Strip searches of visitors, allegedly to make sure that no drugs, weapons or other non-permitted items are being carried into the prison, can be extremely humiliating, adding another level of discomfort to the visiting process. Other difficulties that visitors encounter are changed visiting hours, removal of their names from the list of approved visitors without warning and enduring insulting comments made by prison staff.

The Commission believes that it is important for prisoners to remain close to their immediate and extended families. Family members are often the main source of news and information that keeps the prisoner in touch with the outside world. Visits allow the prisoner to relate to persons who are not prisoners or guards. Family members sometimes can provide financial support to the prisoner while incarcerated and following release. Maintenance of ties to relatives and friends is important to prisoner re-entry into the community following incarceration. It is important, therefore, that guards and other prison staff be helped to understand that the long-term benefits of prisoners maintaining contact with their families outweigh any short-term drawbacks and that families and friends of prisoners should be treated with respect.

Families have various methods of staying in contact with

loved ones who are incarcerated. These include on-site visitation, letter writing and telephone calls. Some prison systems permit furloughs which allow the prisoner to leave the institution to spend time with their family in the community. Seven states allow conjugal visits on prison grounds for prisoners with legal spouses.[82] A few states allow children on extended overnight visits, either in addition to or in lieu of the prisoner's spouse.

The Commission heard testimony and reviewed materials detailing the types of supports that institutions can provide to assist in the maintenance of family linkages. They include: (1) providing individual and family counseling for prisoners and their families, including suggestions for child rearing; (2) explaining the rules, regulations and conditions of prison life to family members so that they can better understand the day-to-day experiences of their incarcerated loved one; (3) arranging individual conferences to discuss areas of crisis and difficulty; (4) facilitating access for the family members of prisoners with social service agencies and other support programs in the community; (5) organizing support groups of spouses and children of prisoners so that persons in similar situations can have the opportunities for discussion.[83]

Considerable attention should be paid to the ties between incarcerated parents and their children. Children are often traumatized by the incarceration of a parent or grandparent and may not want to visit the prison or jail, and the incarcerated parent often feels ashamed and embarrassed. Prison rules often identify the custodial parent as the sole source of approval for a child's visit or the only one who can accompany the child to the prison. If that parent is estranged from the prisoner, approval for the visit may not be granted, even though such a visit would benefit all parties. The Commission believes that any decisions to prohibit parent-child visits should be based on court orders derived from careful study rather than arbitrary prison rules.

To facilitate parent-child contact, some prisons have set up specially-designed visiting areas where prisoners can spend time with their young children in a relaxed, informal environment. The areas often contain children's games, toys and educational materials that can be used for play time activities. These programs can make trips to the prison a more pleasant experience for families and children and increase order in the visiting area.

It is important, however, that these institutional supports to prisoners and their families be offered, but not forced. Frequently, prisoners and their families participate in these programs if the programs include a peer counseling component and are operated by outside agencies rather than prison staff. What is crucial is that support is provided upon request on a timely basis in a way that permits families to maintain some control. Ideally, prison family linkage programs should be collaborative efforts involving prison officials, community professionals, family members and prisoners.

COUNSELING

Many individuals enter prisons having suffered from physical and sexual abuse as children.[84] This is particularly true for women. There is a clear need for prison caseworkers, counselors and other staff to be made aware of and sensitized to the long-term effects of such abuse. While progress has been made in the development of treatment programs for sexual offenders, old stereotypes, attitudes and purely punishment-oriented sentencing still prevails. Because concerns for public safety run particularly high, it takes greater effort to implement focused treatment programs for prisoners convicted of rape or sexual battery.

In establishing counseling programs, it is important to recognize cultural differences. Use of bilingual and bicultural staff and prisoner peer counselors can help prisoners to better understand their circumstances and make necessary life changes. Involvement of community-based organizations and professional agencies may make prisoners more willing to participate in counseling programs. Confidentiality must be maintained so that information shared by prisoners is not used against them by guards or other prisoners.

Some of those incarcerated suffer from mental and emotional illnesses. Counselors and other prison staff should be trained to recognize the symptoms of these illnesses and to make appropriate referrals so that those identified can be diagnosed and treated.

SPIRITUALITY AND SELF-ESTEEM

Prisoners should be encouraged to become involved in self-help and peer-led discussion groups for alcoholism, drug dependency, spousal abuse and other problems. These groups can help prisoners build self-esteem and coping skills. Other prisoner initiatives can include classes and organizations stressing cultural awareness, racial and ethnic history, religious and spiritual beliefs and self-awareness. Prison administrations should be supportive of these efforts and allow prisoners to establish positive leadership cadres.

A particular area of dissension between prison administrations and prisoners over the years has been denial of religious freedom. While mainstream Protestant, Catholic and Jewish religions often are welcomed, prisoners who follow non-Western religions—such as Islam, Buddhism and Native American Spirituality—can face barriers to their religious worship. Meals are served that contain forbidden foods and no alternatives are provided. The Christian Sabbath and holidays are set aside for worship, ignoring the holy days of other faiths. The Commission believes that free access to religion and spirituality is an integral part of the restoration process of individuals in prisons and jails and should not be restricted or denied.

The importance and value of African American, Latino, Native American and Asian American history and culture should be stressed, not only to prisoners and convicted persons but also to guards and other criminal justice system staff. Prison-based affiliates of community-based groups should be established to help build self-esteem and cultural awareness.

VII
INDIVIDUAL AND
COMMUNITY
RESPONSIBILITY

Persons of color comprise both the majority of incarcerated persons as well as the majority of crime victims in the United States. It is indeed a paradox that African American, Latino and Native American communities must suffer this double burden. Yet, the statistics are clear. Assaults, robberies, car thefts, rapes, and drug crimes all take their toll on communities that are already burdened by high unemployment, poor health care, poor housing and high rates of imprisonment.

While there is a tendency to place individuals in one of two categories—criminal or victim—the lines are not so clearly drawn. Studies in Boston and Philadelphia have shown that people who are treated in hospital emergency rooms as the victims of violent crimes often reappear in a court room as the perpetrators of violence.[85] Many of those who are arrested for robbery and burglary have themselves been robbed or had property taken from their homes. In drug-related cases, sons and daughters often steal from their parents or grandparents.

The poorest and most oppressed suffer most from crime and violence in barrios, central cities and on reservations.

One reason street crime is so high in communities of color is because of high unemployment which results in joblessness and idle time, particularly among unskilled and uneducated youth. Another reason is the self-hatred that has emerged as the legacy of a nation that has refused to recognize the history and culture of citizens who are not of European descent. This self-hatred is played out in violent behavior and lack of respect for other persons of color.[86] There is a hopelessness that finds release in excessive concern for material success (legal or illegal), escape into drug and alcohol-induced fantasies, and exercise of coercive physical power through guns, knives and other weapons of destruction.

Therefore, for communities of color, it is important that convicted persons and victims gain an understanding of the commonalities that bind them together in a circle of injustice. One of the ways that this can be done is through careful implementation of programs whereby convicted persons provide restitution to the individuals they have harmed and service to the communities of which they are members. Sometimes this restitution is financial; sometimes convicted persons provide a period of community service, working with young people, community agencies or otherwise serving the needs of community.

Often, victims do not want to have anything to do with the person who robbed or injured them. Yet, for those who are willing to make some connection, there are benefits. As an example, a *Friends* newsletter described a visit by a leader of a victims' advocacy organization who reluctantly agreed to meet with a prisoners' organization inside the institution.

During her visit, "she heard the words she had been wanting to hear since she became a victim of crime herself and began her remarkable career on behalf of crime victims: 'We are sorry, we were wrong in doing what we did, we want to change.'"[87]

RELIGIOUS AND SPIRITUAL GROUPS

Within communities of color, churches and religious organizations can and must play a pivotal role. The task is two-fold: helping individuals within the criminal justice system and mobilizing broader communities to create a system that is truly "just" in its treatment of convicted persons and victims of crime.

Certainly the entire burden should not fall on the religious and spiritual community. However, religious organizations play a special role in African, Latino, Asian and Native American communities. The cultural and spiritual strengths and material resources of these institutions can be used to work with incarcerated individuals and to help men and women make the transition from prison to the outside world and to form bridges of forgiveness within communities of color.

Some churches, mosques, temples and other religious institutions live up to this potential. Others do not, preferring either to ignore incarcerated individuals or to focus entirely on spiritual regeneration without addressing secular issues of family linkage, employment and housing. Religious institutions and groups which accept the responsibility of working with prisoners and ex-prisoners can assist with family visits, support prisoners and their families with educational and counseling programs and provide opportunities for housing and employment after release.

Churches and religious institutions can address the problems of ex-prisoners by providing direct services and by advocating for government and other private support of post-release programs.[88] Local congregations, working collectively across denominational lines or through regional councils, can initiate pastoral counseling services, mentoring programs, life skills training, job search counseling and training, day care programs and other needed services. Support from religious leaders and members of a congregation for a half-way house or a facility for troubled youth or drug treatment center in the neighborhood can help calm community fears. Through their input, community-based programs can be designed that provide support for convicted persons and security for the surrounding residential area. Communities of faith also can support and strengthen existing programs with financial contributions and with the time and energy of members of the community.

It is critical that substantial support for these efforts come from religious and spiritual institutions that are in and of communities of color. Far too often, the only churches providing extensive prison ministries and post-release programs are based in white communities. While such efforts can be helpful, many prisoners of color are often reluctant to become involved in such programs and speak openly and earnestly about the need to connect with spiritual and religious persons from their own ethnic, racial and cultural communities.

Within the prisons and jails, religious and spiritual leaders can mediate conflict between prisoners and staff. These men and women, as a result of their calling, often have the skills and moral standing to work with administrators of criminal justice systems to find ways of improving prison policies and procedures. In their work with individuals, religious and spiritual leaders and lay persons also can help prisoners to move beyond anger and guilt toward reconciliation, restitution and self-worth. If religious and spiritual institutions from communities of color have the will and the commitment, they can be a dynamic part of changing the disillusionment and hopelessness—of convicted persons and of the community—which lead to rejection and recidivism.

COMMUNITY INVOLVEMENT

Even though the criminal justice system has its greatest day-to-day impact on communities of color, there has been little structured response from those communities regarding the need for change. Part of the reason for this is the range of competing interests that call for community involvement. However, another reason is that persons convicted of crimes, particularly poor persons and persons of color, tend to be shunted to the margins of society. Relatively few persons are willing to take the public censure that comes with advocating for prisoners' rights.

The sheer complexity of the criminal justice system, with its myriad of varying jurisdictions and regulations, limits community response. This complexity makes the implementation of fundamental changes in the system quite difficult. Patterns of racism and unfair treatment of prisoners and convicted persons tend to get lost in a multitude of seemingly unconnected individual appeals for redress from specific local, state or federal institutions. The battle lines are predictable: prisoners, their friends, families and prisoners' rights advocates on one side and criminal justice bureaucracies, elected officials, victims of crime and a vocal majority of the general public on the other.

While there have been some victories against the inequities and racism of the criminal justice system, they are not enough. Those enmeshed in the nation's courts, jails and prisons generally are the most unrecognized and the least respected members of society: poor, unemployed, uneducated, non-white and sometimes undocumented. Thus, when they complain about their treatment and their circumstances, their cries are all too often ignored.

Of course, not all criminal behavior is relegated to the underclass. America's prisons also hold individuals from middle and working class families, who received good educations and who had good jobs. However, the stigma associated with incarceration is such that the families and friends of these individuals are reluctant to disclose to the public that they have or had a loved one in prison. Therefore, these individuals, many of whom have considerable standing in their communities, also seek redress from the criminal justice system on an individual basis rather than working in concert with others.

Certainly there has always been some broad-based community response among persons of color to the imperative for changing this nation's response to crime. Various local groups and individuals in African American, Latino, Native American and Asian American communities already are active with penal reform organizations and criminal justice advisory committees. Some grassroots organizations have developed visitation, instructional and other supportive programs for men and women who are incarcerated. (These experiences are reflected in the volunteer service of many members of the Commission.) However, on the whole, the response of communities of color has fallen far short of what would be expected, given the magnitude of the problem.

When communities begin to deal with issues of crime and justice, the focus is generally on "holding criminals accountable" and "making them pay." Unfortunately, there is relatively little attention given to holding society accountable for failing to address the poverty, lack of education and lack of jobs which have paved the way to prison for many persons of color. Much of the anger regarding crime in communities of color is understandable. It stems from frustration with a criminal justice system which rarely allows convicted persons to express the responsibility they have accepted for their crimes. As a result, community anger and despair is often transformed into a call for vengeance, sometimes inflicting equivalent damage on the person convicted of the criminal act.

Unfortunately, there is a tendency to "write off" prisoners and convicted persons, and refuse to accept them back into the community or forgive them for their crimes. This rejection begins when an individual is sentenced to jail or prison and continues after he or she has been released. Some of this rejection by the community stems from a lack of understanding. While many persons of color know someone or are related to someone who has served time for some criminal act, this personal association does not translate into real understanding of the criminal justice system. Other people have never been inside a prison or jail and so have no first-hand knowledge of the conditions. Without recognition of how prisons actually function and the difficulties prisoners face, it is easy to blame the high rates of recidivism on individual failures rather than the criminal justice system's failure as a whole.

The Commission believes that communities of color must become involved in a broad-based way in urging changes in the nation's police, court and prison systems. For this to happen, there must be widespread public education about the real world of sentencing, incarceration and post-release. People must begin to understand the following: (1) if a community refuses to hire ex-prisoners for jobs or allow them to receive welfare grants, the choices left for survival are extremely limited; (2) if a person is deserted by family and friends because of past actions, even when he or she has made every effort to become a better, more productive individual, drugs and alcohol provide an escape from pain and can lead the way back to prison; (3) warehousing individuals without providing positive alternatives for life changes builds anger, resentment and hostility that may well seek a release in violence once the prison doors swing open.

Only when communities of color and other Americans mobilize to make changes in the criminal justice system will there be any possibility of ending the cycle of six out of ten incarcerated persons eventually returning to criminal behavior in the community and, ultimately, returning to life behind prison walls.

VIII
RECOMMENDATIONS FOR ACTION

The fundamental nature of the criminal justice system in the United States, with its foundations in racism, makes it difficult to suggest changes that will make a real difference. However, in its deliberations and discussions, members of the Commission were able to agree on a series of recommended steps that can be taken by communities of color, criminal justice systems, legislators and advocates to improve conditions for all those who suffer as a result of crime.

Even if all of these recommendations were acted on, the criminal justice system would still have fundamental flaws. However, the Commission believes that acting on these recommendations would enable more men, women and children of color to reestablish positive, productive lives.

Community Response

1.   Communities of color, with the assistance of private sector organizations and foundations, must implement a broad-

based information campaign, using media and other out-
reach mechanisms to alert the public to the social, personal
and economic costs of the current criminal justice system.

2.   Persons of color must employ lobbyists and organize to
support legislative strategies for the implementation of
positive changes in the criminal justice system that focus
on the fundamental causes of crime.

3.   Community based organizations, including churches and
other religious institutions, must create additional programs that address social needs in a comprehensive way,
including Saturday schools, mentoring programs, home-
less shelters, drug treatment programs and support groups,
day care centers, parenting programs and recreational
facilities.

Cultural Diversity

4.   Cultural diversity and sensitivity training programs must
be required for persons at all levels of the criminal justice
system, including police, judges, probation and parole
officers and prison guards.

5.   The criminal justice system must employ more persons of
color, including bilingual and cultural men and women, at
all levels.

6.   National organizations that represent persons of color
must develop and disseminate easy-to-read, bilingual and
culturally sensitive brochures and audio-visual materials
that can inform low-literate and/or non-English speaking
persons about the criminal justice system, including bail
arrangements, court procedures, prison regulations and
specifics of probation and parole.

7.   Criminal justice staff must be sensitized and trained to

look at family issues within a cultural context as part of their work with probationers and parolees.

Police

8. Independent monitoring programs and citizen complaint review boards, based in community agencies, must be established and empowered to review and make recommendations on policing, sentencing and other criminal justice components.

Prosecution, Courts and Sentencing

9. State legislatures and/or the federal government must abolish the death penalty as cruel and unusual punishment.

10. Increased funding must be made available from public and private sources to assure fair and adequate defense counsel and appeal opportunities for persons accused of crimes who cannot afford such counsel.

11. A legislative framework must be implemented requiring more individualized sentencing, including increased use of community-based alternatives to incarcerations and less reliance on mandatory sentencing.

12. Family impact studies, which review the potential impact of incarceration on the family of the convicted person, must become a required part of the pre-sentence investigation report that is presented to the judge.

Alternatives to Incarceration

13. The policy of prison expansion must be stopped and resources channeled in new directions: crime prevention, community-based alternatives, educational programs,

housing and access to health care.

14. Convicted persons must be encouraged to provide restitution to victims of crime as part of the process of reconciliation and not as an additional form of punishment that is used to arbitrarily extend or justify imprisonment.

Prison Programs

15. Prisoners must be given meaningful work and be paid a fair wage with funds earned used for victim restitution, family support and individual escrow accounts for post-release.

16. Programs must be established for prisoners and convicted persons which combine education, life survival skills, vocational training and stress management.

17. Prison, probation and parole programs must be designed with input from prisoners and ex-prisoners to assure relevance and maximum cooperation and effectiveness.

18. Accreditation must be mandated for all prisons and alternative programs for convicted persons, including required training for criminal justice staff.

19. National criteria must be developed requiring classification of prisoners based on individual needs.

Post-Release

20. Persons who have been imprisoned must not be discriminated against in employment, housing, education or access to services on the basis of their prior imprisonment.

Drug Treatment and Other Health Care

21. All prisoners must have access to adequate health care services.

22. Drug addiction must be recognized as a public health problem for which incarceration is not the solution.
23. Holistic and cultural-specific drug treatment programs must be established in prisons and jails for prisoners, families of prisoners and guards.
24. Innovative community-based drug abuse centers must be established to meet the needs of individuals addicted to drugs and alcohol.
25. Facilities and treatment programs must be established for convicted persons with mental and emotional illnesses and criminal justice system staff must be trained to more appropriately identify and refer those individuals for appropriate treatment.
26. Persons with AIDS and HIV infection must not be segregated from other prisoners, and workshops must be conducted for prisoners, families of prisoners and prison staff to provide accurate information about AIDS.

Youth

27. Communities of color must initiate programs to reclaim our youth and provide them with a positive value system and a sense of their history and culture through recreational and educational programs that build skills, self-awareness and self-esteem.
28. Community-based groups that work with convicted youth must develop increased self-sufficiency.
29. Juveniles must not be sentenced as adults and placed in adult facilities. Rather, successful programs in juvenile institutions must be strengthened and new programs developed, with an emphasis not on incarceration, but on community-based programming.

30. Appropriate services for juveniles, including programs for alcoholism and addiction to other drugs, must be provided in community-based and residential facilities.

31. Curricula for elementary and secondary school children must incorporate materials on the operations and functions of the criminal justice system, including policing, sentencing, imprisonment and community-based alternatives.

Women

32. Model prison, probation and post-release programs must be established to meet the special needs of incarcerated women, particularly those with dependent children. Effective programs of this type must be identified and replicated.

Political Prisoners

33. The United States government must free its political prisoners.

Refugees and Immigrants

34. The United States government must not continue to detain refugees in prison-like circumstances in violation of international laws.

35. Independent organizations must be allowed to provide factual, relevant presentations to undocumented individuals who are being detained by the United States government so that the detainees and staff of the facilities can better understand the rules of asylum, refugee status and immigration.

36. National organizations that represent persons of color

must develop and disseminate easy-to-read, bilingual and culturally sensitive brochures and audio-visual materials that can inform low-literate and/or non-English speaking persons about the criminal justice system, including bail arrangements, court procedures, prison regulations and specifics of probation and parole.

Religion and Sprituality

37. Counseling programs and discussion groups must be established for prisoners and convicted persons which can help these men and women move beyond feeling ostracized, frustrated, and angry (with the society and family member) to reconciliation.

38. Freedom of religious expression for persons in prison must be recognized and accepted by prison administrators and guards.

39. African American, Latino, Asian American and Native American spiritual and religious leaders must become involved in providing prison ministries, including attention to prisoners' families and post-release programs.

Notes

Foreword

1. Bell, M., *The Turkey Shoot:Tracking the Attica Coverup* (New York:Grover Press, 1985).

2. Bowker, L.H., *Prison Victimization* (New York:Elfevier Publishers, 1980).

3. Mauer, M., "Young Black Men and the Criminal Justice System: A Growing National Problem," *The Sentencing Project* (February 1990).

4. Robert, R.E., Program Director, Inmate Community Program, Sidell, Louisiana, conversation with Haki Madhubuti.

5. Ibid.

Chapter II: Analysis of Crime and Justice in America

6. Mauer, M., "Americans Behind Bars: A Comparison of International Rates of Incarceration," *The Sentencing Project* (January 1991).

7. Murphy, J., New York State Coalition for Criminal Justice, testimony at Philadelphia hearings of the National Commission on Crime and Justice (June 1990).

8. Rocawich, L., "Lock Em Up: America's all-purpose cure for crime." *Progressive* (August 1987).

9. For a description of Anti-Asian immigration laws, see *U.S. Commission on Civil Rights, Tarnished Golden Door: Issues in Immigration*, Chapters 1 and 2, 1980.

10. Bellecourt, C., Statement by Commissioner at Atlanta Hearings of the National Commissions on Crime and Justice, September 1990.

11. Aiyetoro, A., National Prison Project (testimony at Philadelphia hearings of the National Commission on Crime and Justice), June 1990.

12. National Institute of Justice, *Sourcebook of Criminal Justice Statistics*, 1989.

13. Gardner, C., *Aid to Imprisoned Mothers* (testimony at Atlanta hearings of the National Commissions on Crime and Justice), September 1990.

14. Mauer, M., "Americans Behind Bars," op. cit.

15. Parker, A., "Crimes of Punishment: At the Door to Reform of the Criminal Justice," *Sojourner* (June 1990).

Chapter III: Structure of the Criminal Justice System

16. Hall, D., "Community Policing: An Overview of the Literature," *Public Policy Report,* New York State Division of Criminal Justice Services, Office of Justice Systems Analysis, 1990.

17. Ibid.

18. Pickens, J., Atlanta Criminal Defense and Justice Project (testimony at Atlanta hearings of the National Commission on Crime and Justice), September 1990.

19. Route, C., National Association of Former Prisoners (testimony at Atlanta hearings of the National Commission on Crime and Justice), September 1990.

20. Judges Braxton, J. and Gordon, L., panelist remarks at Philadelphia hearings of the National Commission on Crime and Justice, June 1990; Judges Cooper, C. and Hopewell, A., panelist remarks at Atlanta hearings of the National Commission on Crime and Justice, September 1990.

21. American Friends Services Committee, "Facts on Alternatives to Incarceration," Factsheet, 1990.

22. Ibid.

23. Green, A., Personal correspondence from Commission member, April 1991.

24. Rocawich, L., Op. cit.

25. Murphy, J., Op. cit.

26. Esteves, A., "Electronic Incarceration in Massachusetts: A Critical Analysis." *Social Justice*, Vol. 17, No. 4.

27. "Facts on Alternatives to Incarceration," Op. cit.

28. McDonald, D., "Restitution and Community Service," *Crime File Study Guide*, National Institute of Justice, 1990.

29. Rocawich, L., Op. cit.

30. Mauer, M., "Americans Behind Bars," Op. cit.

31. Parker, A., Op. cit.

32. Mauer, M., "Americans Behind Bars," Op. cit.

33. Aiyetoro, A., Op. cit.

34. Isikoff, M., "Does Inmate Labor Work?" *Washington Post*, (November 11, 1990).

35. Pickens, J., Op. cit.

36. Eagleston, W., Testimony at Philadelphia hearings of the National Commission on Crime and Justice, June 1990.

37. Ibid.

38. American Friends Services Committee, *Lessons of Marion-The Failure of a Maximum Security Prison: A History and Analysis, with Voices of Prisoners*, 1985.

39. Owens, D. (former Commissioner of Corrections), Commonwealth of Pennsylvania, Testimony at Philadelphia hearings of the National Commission on Crime and Justice, June 1990.

40. Sutton, C., "Street Time: Probation and Parole in Pennsylvania," *Philadelphia New Observer*, 1990.

Notes

41. Route, C. and Ealy, A., Testimony at Atlanta hearings of the National Commission on Crime and Justice, September 1990.

42. Shepard, S., Murder Victims' Families for Reconciliation (discussion with Commission Staff), May 1991.

43. National Coalition to Abolish the Death Penalty.

44. Gross, S. E., *A Sage of Shame: Racial Discrimination and the Death Penalty*, 1990.

Chapter IV: Impact of Drugs

45. Murphy, J., Op. cit.

46. National Institute of Justice, "Drug Use Forecasting," 1989 Annual Report, (June 1990).

47. Shannon, E., "A Losing Battle," *Time* (December 3, 1990).

48. Murphy, J., Op. cit.

49. Ibid.

50. National Commission on AIDS Report, "HIV Disease in Correctional Institutions" (March 1991).

Chapter V: Special Populations

51. Ibid.

52. McConney, N., Testimony at Philadelphia hearings of the National Commission on Crime and Justice, June 1990.

53. National Commission on AIDS, Op. cit.

54. Parker, A., Op. cit.

55. National Commissions on AIDS, Op. cit.

56. American Friends Services Committee, "Facts on Women in Prison," *Factsheet*, 1990.

57. National Commissions on AIDS, op. cit.

58. Herrick, S., Amnesty International (testimony at Atlanta hearings of the National Commission on Crime and Justice), September 1990.

59. Ibid.

60. Ibid.

61. Ibid.

62. Tamayo, W., Personal correspondence from Commission member, April 18, 1991.

63. Nieves, E., Personal correspondence from Commission member, May 10, 1991.

64. Interfaith Prisoners of Conscience Project brochure, National Council of Churches, 1991.

65. Special International Tribunal on the Violation of Human Rights of Political Prisoners and Prisoners of War in United States Prisons and Jails, December 1990.

66. Ibid.

67. Ibid.

68. Ibid.

69. National Commission on AIDS, Op. cit.

70. Ibid.

71. Survey of Federal Bureau of Corrections Staff, National Institute of Justice/Bureau of Justice Statistics, 1988.

72. Letts, S. Delaware Council on Crime and Justice (testimony before the National Commission on AIDS), 1990.

73. National Commission on AIDS, Op. cit.

Chapter VI: Support Programs

74. Ibid.

75. Bell, R., "Prison Schools Need a New Curriculum," *Philadelphia Inquirer* (October 19, 1990).

76. National Commission on AIDS, Op. cit.

77. Ibid.

78. Office of Minority Health, U.S. Department of Health & Human Services, 1990.

79. National Commission on AIDS, op. cit.

80. Ibid.

81. Corbean, S. and Power, P., "Role of the Family in the Rehabilitation of the Offender," *Institutional Journal of Offender Therapy and Comparative Criminology.*

82. Buchanon and Unger, "Impact of Long-Term Confinement on Offenders' Family and Friends," *Long-Term Offender Report* (Bureau of Justice statistics), 1990.

83. Finney Hairston, C., "Children's Visiting Programs in Prison," Indiana University School of Social Work, 1990.

84. Legesse, E., Philadelphia prison warden (testimony at Philadelphia hearings of the National Commission on Crime and Justice), June 1990.

Chapter VII: Individual and Community Responsibility

85. Schwartz, D., Children's Hospital of Philadelphia interview, August 1989.

86. Wilson, A., *Black on Black Violence: The Psychodynamics of Black Self-Annihilation in Service of White Domination* (New York: AfroWorld Info Systems, 1990).

87. Monthly Newsletter, *Scarsdale Friends Meeting*, No. 9 (December 1990).